Course Manual

for

CORNERSTONE
Building on Your Best

Rhonda J. Montgomery
The University of Nevada, Las Vegas

Patricia G. Moody
The University of South Carolina

Robert M. Sherfield
Community College of Southern Nevada

Allyn and Bacon
Boston · London · Toronto · Sydney · Tokyo · Singapore

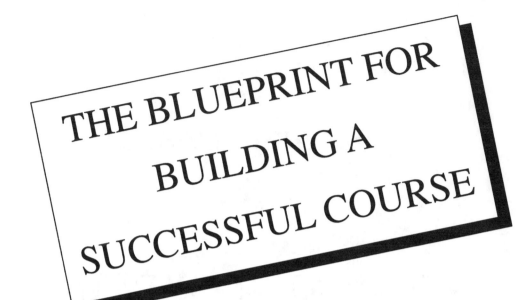

THE BLUEPRINT FOR BUILDING A SUCCESSFUL COURSE

Copyright © 1997 by Allyn & Bacon
A Viacom Company
Needham Heights, Massachusetts 02194

Internet: www.abacon.com
America Online: keyword: College Online

ISBN 0-205-26276-2

Printed in the United States of America

10 9 8 7 6 5 4 3 2 1   01 00 99 98 97 96

TABLE OF CONTENTS

ACTIVITIES QUICK REFERENCE

To The Instructor

Cornerstone is intended to be a self-discovery text for the student. It is filled with activities that will allow students to apply what they have learned in each chapter. At the beginning of each chapter, the activity called "At This Moment" will help the students assess where their abilities lie in dealing with the subject matter at hand. After each of these activities, discussions should take place to allow the student to focus on the material in the chapter. The discussions should provide lively conversations among students as they share their personal stories of tragedy and triumph.

We have arranged the chapters in a logical sequence, but do not feel as if you have to follow the text chapter-by-chapter. If the format does not work for you, use your own. This manual is intended to give you a framework or blueprint of ideas and suggestions that may assist you in providing the students with activities, journal writing, through-provoking situations and group activities. You will probably have many more activities than the ones in this manual. Use them to your best advantage. After all, this manual is nothing without you.

Some instructors feel as if they have to give tests in the course. For this reason, we have included quiz suggestions for each chapter in the book. If you do not feel comfortable using these suggestions, skip them or make up your own. You will be the best judge in determining how your students should be evaluated.

We would love to have your ideas and suggestions for making this text and manual more effect for you and your students. We invite your feedback and welcome your comments. At the end of this manual, you will find sheets for use in submitting ideas for activities for our next edition. We would be happy to list your name and your institution's name in the acknowledgements of upcoming editions.

Rhonda, Pat and Robb

WE'RE HERE FOR YOU!

Our dedication and commitment to the Cornerstone Program does not end with your adoption. As a matter of fact, we feel that our commitment has just begun! We want you to know that we can address your questions, help you solve problems, offer advice and provide support to you through several mechanisms. We're here for you and your institution.

VISIT OUR WEB SITE

Cornerstone: Building on Your Best, is now on the World Wide Web. We invite you to visit. Our address is: **http://www.abacon.com** Click on Freshman Orientation.

WRITE TO US DIRECTLY

We welcome your comments and questions. Write to us directly on America Online at:

Rhonda J. Montgomery	rmontgo@aol.com
Patricia G. Moody	pgmoody@aol.com
Robert M. Sherfield	rsherfield@aol.com

This seminar is designed to help you prepare for teaching the first-year college experience course.

The philosophy behind the seminar is that instructors need to thoroughly understand the vital role they play in motivating, stimulating, and ensuring student success in the first year and beyond. The presenters believe that if instructors can develop better teaching skills in these areas and understand all of the resources at their disposal, they will be able to construct the best possible course for their particular institution.

Workshop participants will be actively involved in hands-on exercises, topical discussions, and projects. This workshop will also provide participants opportunities to share ideas, suggestions, syllabi, activities, evaluations, chapter plans, and teaching strategies to be used in the classroom setting.

Whether your goal is fostering academic excellence or just keeping students in college—whether you are a first-time instructor or have taught first-year orientation courses for years, you will benefit from this seminar.

Group Dynamics/Cooperative Learning
- How do I build a team for student success?
- How do I network with and get help from my colleagues?
- How do I make a group work effectively?
- How do I manage group conflict?

Maximizing Teaching Materials
- Using activities as discovery tools
- Using assessment tools for positive change
- Using journal keeping to introduce social and cultural issues
- Tips for improving your teaching/communication style
- Ways to initiate lively discussions

- To test, or not to test. . . a personal decision
- Globalizing through Internet activities
- Using student stories as examples
- Effective use of video for lecture enhancement
- How to best use Transparency masters

Teaching Across the Curriculum
- How to tailor your teaching to a diverse student population
- How to personalize your freshman orientation program to specific curricula
- How to use faculty and staff as "experts in residence"

Empowering Students & Critical Thinking
- Teaching students to think critically across the curriculum
- Teaching students to transfer knowledge
- Academic success beyond the freshman orientation class

Classroom "Action" Research
- How to track student success and document the importance of the freshman orientation course to your college or university
- How to use your orientation course to keep students in college
- How to conduct valuable classroom evaluations

Your Role as Advisor and Counselor
- Becoming a mentor
- Facilitating peer advisement and counseling
- Working with your advisement and counseling center
- Advising about communication styles and stress management

Career Planning
- How to develop a career assessment plan for your students
- How to use a variety of instruments in the freshman orientation course:
    1. Myers Briggs Type Inventory
    2. Holland Self-directed Search
    3. Dictionary of Occupational Titles
    4. The Occupational Outlook Handbook
    5. The Coopersmith Self-esteem Inventory
- Effective ways to work with your campus career center

Resources Available from Allyn & Bacon for the Course

Customized syllabi and booklets specific to your institution; Course Manuals; Double-Entry Journals; Videos; Faculty Newsletters; Academic Supplements on Money Management, Cyber Literacy, and English as a Second Language; a Freshman Orientation website and more!

Questions and Discussion

For more information about this training program, contact your local Allyn and Bacon Representative or visit the Allyn & Bacon Website <http://www.abacon.com>.

IDEAS FOR PLANNING THE COURSE

Research indicates that students who enroll in first-year orientation courses "have a higher probability of returning for the sophomore year" (Fidler, P., The University of South Carolina). Further studies at The University of South Carolina, the site for the Center for the Study of the Freshman Year Experience, were reported in a 1987 article, "Who We Are, What We Do, What We've Accomplished" by Jerome Jewler. They found that first year students who enroll in an orientation course tend to exceed their predicted grade point ratio and survive the freshman year at a greater rate than first year students who did not take the course. Student orientation courses can offer success for the student, the faculty member and the college as a whole. With this in mind, you will want to design a course in a format with which you are most comfortable and one that meets the specific needs of students at YOUR institution. Some suggestions for the design may include:

■ **LECTURE**
  While this format is not new, there will probably be a limited amount of lecture in this course. Some of the subject matter will be new to the students and you will need to present it to them in a lecture format. We suggest that no more than 25% of the course be in the lecture format.

■ **SELF-DISCOVERY**
  This text is enriched with activities and questions that should allow students to "feel their way" through the course. They should be allowed to make mistakes, ask questions of themselves and others and experiment with new ideas.

■ **EXERCISES**
  This manual and the text include a wide variety of activities and exercises intended for the individual student, groups and the entire class. We have found that students enjoy the exercises that enhance the chapter material more than any other activity.

■ **GUEST SPEAKERS**
  A powerful tool in a freshman orientation class can be qualified and enlightening guest speakers. We have found that students listen, with great interest, to OTHER students who have gone through certain experiences. It is helpful to pull in people from the community, the college and the student body.

- **FIELD TRIPS**
  This course should be the student's "Window To The World." Field trips to local, state, regional and national points of interest have been identified as educational and memorable by former students. The trips seem to build relationships, promote responsibility, increase awareness and develop cultural appreciation.

- **COOPERATIVE LEARNING**: Our classes spend approximately 50% of the course in group discussion and group discovery exercises. Former students have suggested that they learned the most and enjoyed the material more when it was presented in a discussion/discovery format.

- **MOVIES / VIDEOS:** There are many videos and movies on the market (or for rent) which will add dimension to your class and enhance your lecture. Often, movies can prompt discussion that would otherwise be missed. We have included suggestions for movies and videos at the end of each chapter discussion. You will want to preview our suggestions for content and appropriateness before showing them to your classes.

- **QUIZZES:** As mentioned earlier, some faculty feel as if the course needs quizzes and for this reason, we have included suggestions for chapter quizzes at the end of each unit.

- Allyn & Bacon Video Series: Several videos are available with the Cornerstone Program. The first video: "Building on Your Best" is intended for use as a motivational, discussion-generating video best shown early in the course. It is available free of charge to client schools.

  The remaining videos in the Allyn & Bacon Video Series are available at discounted prices to client schools and cover such topics as AIDS, date rape, and study skills topics.

  Each video is designed to promote discussion and discovery in your class. For more information about videos available, contact your local Allyn & Bacon representative or visit the Allyn & Bacon website <www.abacon.com>

WEB SITE RESOURCES TO CONSIDER WHILE BUILDING YOUR COURSE

http://www.mukc.edu/cctr/dept/cad/nade.htm
The National Association of Developmental Education

http://www.mcli.dist.maricopa.edu/events/crla/
The College Reading and Learning Association

http://www.acs.appstate.edu/-rudderbj/kellogg.html
The National Center for Developmental Education

http://www.umkc.edu.cctr/dept/cad/si.htm
The Center for Supplemental Education

http://trio.ume.maine.edu/-nceoa/nceoa.html
TRIO Programs

http://tikkun.ed.asu.edu.aera/home.html
The American Educational Research Association

http://www.pbs.org/mathline/nctmhome.html
The National Council of Teachers of Mathematics

http://www.ncte.org/index.html
The National Council of Teachers of English

http://listserver.literacy.upenn.edu
The National Center on Adult Literacy

http://lcweb.loc.gov/
The Library of Congress

http://ericir.syr.edu/
Ask ERIC Home Page

http://www.schooledu.swt.edu/Whole.Language.html
The Whole Language College Reading Program

http://www.edunet.com/english/grammar/indes.html
On-Line English Grammar

http://www.ed.uiuc.edu/EdPsy-387/Rongchang-Li/esl/indes.html
English as a Second Language

http://jaguar.dacc.cc.il.us/-ramage/disted.html
The Distance Education Homepage

http://homepage.interaccess.com/-ghoyle/
Distance Learning on the Web

http://www skypoint.com/subscribers/jackp/survive.htm/
On-Line Tutoring for How to Survive in College

Gopher: gopher.ed.gov
U.S. Department of Education

Gopher: chronicle.merit.edu
The Chronicle of Higher Education

Many curriculum specific site addresses can be found in the book, ***The Student's Guide to the Internet*** by David Clark (1995) Alpha Books.

COMMON CHAPTER FEATURES

Each unit and chapter is designed with common elements to assist the student in discovery, discussion and exploration. Before each of the four units, we have included actual stories and photos from students across the nation addressing issues to be discussed in the unit. Each unit opener also contains one Internet activity addressing a broad issue of the unit.

Each chapter contains:

■ **SITUATIONAL STORIES**
Each chapter begins with a story about a current or former student. Stories are related to the content of the chapter. Each story can be used to begin discussion on the chapter.

■ **CHAPTER OBJECTIVES**
Each chapter contains learning objectives. These are intended to allow the student to see what will be discussed and discovered in the chapter.

■ **AT THIS MOMENT**
This activity is intended to assess where the student stands on information to be presented in the chapter. This activity can also be used to prompt discussion.

■ **EXERCISES**
We have included a wide array of activities in each chapter to aid in self-discovery, discussion and facilitation by the instructor. Additional activities are also included in this manual.

■ **CORNERSTONES**
At the end of each section or chapter, we have included the "cornerstones" or tips for building success in particular areas of interest. These are provided to assist the student in developing stronger coping skills.

■ **ILLUSTRATIONS**
A cast of "characters" is introduced in the front of the Double Entry Journal. Throughout the text, they comment on life from the student's perspective using humor, sarcasm and cutting honesty. The illustrations were conceived and drawn by an actual college student.

■ **ONE MINUTE JOURNAL**
At the end of each chapter, you will find a brief journal entry to be completed by the student in one minute or less. This is intended to assist the student in assessing what was learned in the chapter.

■ **QUESTIONS**
Each chapter has a variety of questions intended to assist the student in self-discovery. Some of the questions are "easy" or simple while others will require a great deal of thought, maybe even over night or over the weekend.

■ **QUOTES**
Each chapter begins with a quote of interest to the material found in the chapter. Quotes are also scattered throughout the chapter to reinforce stories, situations and subject matter.

■ **QUIZZES**
The Course Manual has suggested chapter quiz items for each chapter found in the text. You will find quiz suggestions for Essay and Application questions.

Each Unit contains:

■ **PART OPENERS**
Each unit opens with testimonies and photos of two students from across the country commenting on the content of the unit and their experiences dealing with the subject mater at hand.

■ **INTERNET ACTIVITIES**
At the end of each unit, an Internet activity is included and is designed to complement the unit's subject matter The activity will assist the student in using the Internet and exploring cyber-possibilities.

A shrink-wrapped supplement to Cornerstone free to the student is the Double Entry Journal.

■ **DOUBLE ENTRY JOURNAL**
An additional supplement packaged with Cornerstone is the Double Entry Journal. It is intended to open the lines of communication between student and teacher and prompt discussion. Some of the journal entries parallel the chapter contents and some are "free" or unrelated to the content. An example of a student/teacher journal is found in the front of the Double Entry Journal.

INDIVIDUAL CHAPTER DESCRIPTIONS

Each chapter has been designed to assist the student in learning specific material while building reading, researching, critical thinking and discussion skills.

UNIT ONE:
Laying A Strong Foundation

PART OPENER I

CHAPTER ONE
Nothing Stays the Same: *Preparing for and Dealing With Change*

Students are asked to assess what part change plays in their daily lives and in their stability. They are given the opportunity to determine how important college is to them and how different college is from high school. This chapter exposes them to the Change Anxiety Wheel, The Change Pie Chart and The Cornerstones for Dealing With Change.

CHAPTER TWO
Planning Your Dreams: *Motivation and Goal Setting*

This chapter, one of the most important in the text, will ask students to evaluate their motivation level and discover motivators in their lives. They will also learn the importance of goals and how to set long and short term goals.

CHAPTER THREE
Outside Looking In: *Building Positive Self-Esteem*

At the end of this chapter, students will be able to define self-esteem, determine why self-esteem is important and use the cornerstones for developing a more positive self-image.

CHAPTER FOUR
Understanding Differences: *A Celebration of Diversity*

While some texts deal with Cultural Diversity, this chapter takes a different road and addresses not only other cultures and sub-cultures, but attitudes that affect our relationships with other people. This chapter is more self-discovery than lecture.

INTERNET ACTIVITY: How Well Do You Understand Yourself?

UNIT TWO:
Sharpening The Tools of Life

PART OPENER II

CHAPTER FIVE
So Much To Do, So Little Time To Do It: *Priority Management*

This chapter is essential in helping the student cope with the daily schedule of college life. Within this chapter are hints, suggestions and plans for learning how to manage time more effectively.

CHAPTER SIX
I Heard You! I Heard You! What Did You Say? *The Art of Active Listening.*

We cannot assume that college students are effective listeners. This chapter is included to assist the student in learning how to become a more active listener and then be able to transfer those skills to the classroom to become a more effective note taker.

CHAPTER SEVEN
Will This Be On The Test?: *The Essentials of Note- Taking*

This chapter gives the students a chance to explore a variety of note taking techniques and strategies. Not only does it address techniques, but also specific methods to improve note taking.

CHAPTER EIGHT
Avoiding the All-nighter: *Studying for Success*

This chapter gives specific methods to improve study skills such as the SQ3R, VCR3, READ Method and using Mnemonics.

CHAPTER NINE
The Proving Ground: *Strategies for Test Taking*

Almost every student in the nation has some degree of test anxiety. This chapter guides the student through activities and exercises that build test-taking skills. Strategies for taking each type of test from essay to multiple choice are given. Sample tests are also included.

INTERNET ACTIVITY: Be Honest With Yourself!

UNIT THREE:
Building The Body, Mind and Soul

PART OPENER III

CHAPTER TEN
Getting Along with Others: *The Power of Relationships*

This chapter deals with the ever-changing life of a college student with regards to relationships. It suggests ways to evaluate the "community" from which you came and the "community" in which you would like to be a member. It is an honest look at friendships, dating, sexuality, harassment, and rape.

CHAPTER ELEVEN
Staying Fit: *A Personal Plan for Wellness*

This chapter allows the student to assess their own health status, discusses key issues in becoming a more healthy person, identifies ways to develop a healthy diet and incorporate an activity schedule into their lives.

CHAPTER TWELVE
I'm Stressed, You're Stressed, We're All Stressed: *Controlling Stress*

One of the most detrimental problems facing college students is their stress level. Some have left home for the first time, some have never had to face difficult classes and some do not know how to deal with anxiety. This chapter discusses the different types of stressors and gives tips and advice for lowering the stress level.

CHAPTER THIRTEEN
Sex, Drugs and Rock and Roll: *Social and Personal Responsibility*

This chapter deals with the day-to-day discussions students must make about alcohol, drugs and experimenting with them. It offers suggestions for help is someone might be abusing drugs. It also offers suggestions for helping peers who are addicted.

INTERNET ACTIVITY: Date Rape: Fact of Fiction?

UNIT FOUR:
The Nuts and Bolts of College Life

PART OPENER IV

CHAPTER FOURTEEN
To Join or Not to Join...That Is the Question: *Co- and Extra Curricular Activities*

Each college student will be faced with the decision of joining a club, organization, fraternity or sorority during their college years. This chapter assists the student in making informed, logical decisions about joining clubs and organizations on campus.

CHAPTER FIFTEEN
What Are You Doing For The Rest Of Your Life? *Career Planning*

An important aspect of a freshman orientation course is assisting student to focus on a major or career. While some students will have already chosen a career path, others will not. This chapter includes activities and discussions about career choices and future plans.

APPENDIX
Things You Need To Know, But Probably Will Never Ask: *Hard Questions, Simple Answers*

The appendix can be used as a chapter or a resource for students. Topics discussed deal with the everyday happenings on the campus such as parking, tuition, decoding professors, financial aid, making out a schedule and registering.

GLOSSARY
Collegeze: *The Language of Success in College*

The Glossary is filled with helpful terms and definitions used by faculty, administrator and students on a daily basis. Included are over 100 terms.

INTERNET ACTIVITY: Great Idea!

PLANNING THE SYLLABUS

Every college in the nation is required to offer students a syllabus on the first day of class. Your syllabus is a binding document between you and your student. It should be taken seriously and much thought should be given to what you want to accomplish and what you want your students to achieve. We have provided a sample syllabi but you will always want to personalize your own.

What Should Be Included?

The contents of your syllabus may be determined by your department or college. In reviewing syllabi from various colleges across the nation, we have found the following items to be universal:

- Instructor's name
- Hours of class meetings and class location
- Office hours and phone number of instructor
- Course Description
- Course Philosophy and Rationale
- Course Objectives
- Instructional Methodology
- Required Text
- Supplemental Materials or text
- Evaluative Methods
- Attendance Policy
- Requirements of the course
- Course outline and calendar

BUILDING THE SYLLABUS

When deciding what materials to include in your course, you may want to try several variations before deciding on one format over another.

Course Outline
45 Sessions @ 3x/wk @ 50 min/session

Class 1

Lecture:	Course Overview
Lecture:	Text Overview
Exercise:	Introduction of class
Exercise:	NAMO

Class 2

Lecture:	Chapter One, Preparing for and Dealing with Change
Exercise:	At This Moment
Exercise:	Forced Choices
Discussion:	Why is College Important
Discussion:	How do College Professor Differ from High School Teachers

Class 3

Discussion:	What is Success
Exercise	If I Could...
Lecture:	Coping with change
Exercise:	Change Anxiety Scale
Discussion:	Twelve Point Plan for Dealing with Change

Class 4

Lecture:	Motivation
Exercise:	At This Moment
Exercise:	Internet Heros
Discussion:	Why is Motivation Important
Discussion:	Cornerstones of Motivation

Class 5

Discussion:	Goal Setting
Lecture:	Evaluation Plan for Goals
Exercise:	Writing Short Term Goals
Exercise:	Goal Partners
Exercise:	Goals Collage
Discussion:	Sharing with the class

Class 6

Exercise:	Writing Long Term Goals
Discussion:	Sharing with the class
Speaker:	Why Goals Are Important

Class 7

Lecture:	Self Esteem
Exercise:	At This Moment
Exercise:	I Am Responsible
Discussion:	Why is it important to develop positive self-esteem?

Class 8

Exercise:	I Am Responsible !
Exercise:	Tackling My Fears.

Class 9

Lecture:	Understanding Differences
Exercise:	At This Moment
Exercise:	Multi-cultural Work Experience
Discussion:	Celebrating our commonalities

Class 10

    Exercise: The Cultural Event (Student Reports)

Class 11

    Movie: Do The Right Thing

Class 12

    Movie: (Cont.) Do The Right Thing

Class 13

    Lecture: Why Priority Management is Important
    Exercise: At This Moment
    Discussion: How Do You Manage Your Time/ Where Does Time Go?

Class 14

    Discussion: Making Time for College - Time to Study - Time for Friends
    Exercise: Scheduling your Time
    Exercise: Making A List
    Exercise: Priority Choices

Class 15

    Lecture: Developing a Calendar for College
    Lecture: Getting Organized
    Exercise: Daily Plan

Class 16

    Lecture: Why is Listening Important
    Exercise: At This Moment
    Lecture: Types of Listening
    Exercise: Circles and Lines
    Exercise: Cabbie
    Exercise: The Accident

Class 17

Lecture:	How to Become a More Effective Listener
Exercise:	Visual Listening
Exercise:	I Can Name That Tune...
Exercise:	Whispers

Class 18

Lecture:	Why is Note Taking Important?
Speaker:	A Guest Lecturer (Student about the importance of note taking)
Exercise:	Passages
Exercise:	The Cornell Method
Exercise:	The Mapping Method
Exercise:	Outlining

Class 19

Exercise:	Note Taking Lab

Class 20

Lecture	Study Skills
Exercise:	At This Moment
Exercise:	Finding a Study Plan
Exercise:	Using Mnemonics
Lecture:	Supplies, Organization, Study Environment

Class 21

Lecture:	SQ3R, READ and Mnemonics
Exercise:	Long Term Memory Check
Lecture:	Test Taking Strategies

Class 22

Exercise:	SQ3R Lab

Class 23

Exercise:	Mnemonics Lab

Class 24
    Lecture: Taking Essay, Multiple Choice, T/False, Short Answer Tests
    Exercise: Sample Chapter Tests

Class 25
    Lecture: Getting Along With Other...Relationships
    Exercise   At This Moment
    Exercise   HIV Encounter
    Discussion: How did HIV Encounter make you feel?

Class 26
    Discussion: A Personal Plan for Wellness
    Exercise: At This Moment
    Exercise: Grocery Store Field trip

Class 27
    Exercise: Fitness Center Tour

Class 28
    Lecture: Why is Wellness Important and Stress Management
    Exercise: At This Moment
    Exercise: Relaxation #1
    Discussion: What Do You Do To Remain Healthy?

Class 29
    Lecture: How can Stress Effect Your Studies
    Exercise: Relaxation #2

Class 30
    Lecture: Sex, Drugs and Rock and Roll
    Exercise: At This Moment
    Exercise: Drinking Diary

Class 31
    Speaker: Director of Campus Health Facility or Doctor

Class 32

Discussion:	Campus Activities
Exercise:	At This Moment
Exercise:	Exploration

Class 33

Speaker:	Campus Activities Director

Class 34

Project:	Student Reports on Activities

Class 35

Project:	Student Reports on Activities

Class 36

Lecture:	Careers
Exercise	Career Research Brainstorming
Exercise	Test Your Perceptions

Class 37

Speaker:	Director of the Career Center

Class 38

Speaker:	CEO or Executive of major Industry or Business

Class 39

Exercise:	Volunteer Brainstorming
Project:	Student Reports on Careers

Class 40

Project:	Student Reports on Careers

Class 41

    Speaker: Open

Class 42

    Lecture: Your College Experience... What has the first semester taught you?

Class 43

    Discussion: Tragedy and Triumph ; Student Questions Solved

Class 44

    Tour: The Campus Career Center

Class 45

    Final Exam

This format can be altered to a twice per week schedule for 45 sessions; once per week for 45 sessions or any configuration your school schedule demands.

SAMPLE COURSE SYLLABUS

COLLEGE SKILLS 101

SPRING, 1996
Monday & Wednesday Classes

OFFICE LOCATION: 2412-D   CHEYENNE CAMPUS
OFFICE PHONE: 555-5555
HOME PHONE: 555-5555

OFFICE HOURS:

Monday	9:30-11:30
Tuesday	8:30- 9:30
Wednesday	9:30-11:30
Thursday	8:30- 9:30

Friday and other hours by appointment

COURSE DESCRIPTION:

This course is designed to assist the student in obtaining academic skills and knowledge necessary to reach his/her educational objective. Topics to be covered include memory development, time management, test-taking, communication skills, career planning, study skills and techniques, questioning skills, ideas for Wellness, an understanding of diversity, and career issues that face many college students. This courses is recommended for all new students, returning students and others who may benefit.

COURSE GOALS:

It is the objective of College 101 to give students training and experiences that will allow them to be successful in their first year and beyond. *The purpose of this course is to provide you the opportunity to learn and adopt methods that promote your success in college and life.*

COURSE OBJECTIVES:

By the end of the semester, students will be able to:

A.   Discuss how you are responsible for your experience in college.

B.   Describe ways you can create a successful experience in college.

C.   List, describe, and use specific methods to:
1.   Improve the ability to recall information
2.   Manage time more efficiently
3.   Read a textbook with improved retention
4.   Prepare for and take tests successfully

5. Take effective notes
6. Present clear reports, both written and verbal
7. Listen, with comprehension, to a lecture
8. Develop stronger and healthier relationships
9. Deal with stress
10. Understand the effects of drugs and alcohol
11. Learn more about extra- and co-curricular activities
12. Develop a philosophy of career development

D. Match resources that are available on campus and in the community that can assist you with problems related to health, academics, personal relationships, discrimination, substance abuse, library research, course changes, part time work, financial aid, social issues, etc.

E. Locate and utilize a variety of library services and resource materials

F. Describe and utilize a model of communication that is effective for sending and receiving information

G. Examine personal ideas and decisions regarding issues typically faced by college students such as personal relationships, drug abuse, health related practices and budgeting money

INSTRUCTIONAL METHODOLOGY:
Because of the interactive nature of this course, a variety of instructional methodology will be used including, but not limited to: lecture, group discussion, group activities, video tapes, guest speakers, field trips, and exploration activities.

REQUIRED TEXT AND SUPPORT MATERIALS:
1. Montgomery, R., Moody, P., & Sherfield, R. (1997) *Cornerstone: Building on Your Best.* Boston: Allyn and Bacon.

2. Double-entry journal

3. A college catalog

4. An open mind, a hearty spirit and a sense of humor

ATTENDANCE POLICY:
Realizing that student success in college is largely dependent on attending class, it is imperative that you make an effort to attend every class. There is no such thing as an excused absence. On certain occasions, circumstances may arise such as sickness, family issues, child care, hospitalization, and unavoidable transportation problems. In that light, students are

allowed to miss no more than 10% of the total class sessions. For COL-101, this translates to 3 classes. Students missing more than 3 classes will receive an "F" for the course.

SPECIAL NOTE #1: If you exceed the number of absences and decide not to speak with the instructor regarding problems or decide not to return to class, it is YOUR responsibility to withdraw from the course. If your name is on the grade roster at the end of the term, a grade of "F" will be recorded.

SPECIAL NOTE #2: Classes begin at the exact times specified in the schedule of classes. If you are tardy twice, it will be counted as an absence. Six **tardies** will result in your reaching the total number of allowed **absences**.

EVALUATION AND GRADING SCALE:

During the course of the semester, you will have the opportunity to earn 2000 points through a variety of exercises, journal activities, presentations, tests and other projects. For your information and convenience, the grading scale is provided below:

2000-1850	—	A	Superior College Level Work
1849-1700	—	B	Above Average College Level Work
1699-1550	—	C	Average Level College Work
1549-1400	—	D	Questionably Unacceptable College Work
1399-below	—	F	Unacceptable College Level Work

Points will be earned as follows:

Journal Entry	8 @ 100 points each	800 Total
Tests	2 @ 100 points each	200 Total
Projects/Exercises	6 @ 100 points each	600 Total
Final Project (Exam)	1 @ 200 points	200 Total
Attendance/Exercises	Various	200 Total
		2000 Total

There are NO curves. Your grade is reflective of your efforts and achievements. If you are absent on the day of an assigned project or exercise, you will not be allowed to make up that exercise unless prior notice or a medical note is given. You operational calendar details when projects are due. I will remind you in class, therefore, **late work is not accepted.**

CLASSROOM ACTIVITIES:

Below, you will find details concerning each of your projects.

Journal Entry Submissions: There will be 8 Journal entries made during the semester. Topics and due date will be assigned in class. Each journal will be scored based on content, grammar and effort. A minimum of three columns will be required for each journal.

Tests: Each student is required to take two unit examinations during the semester. Each test will cover a variety of materials discussed in class and found in your readings. You will be given at least one weeks notice before an exam. Exam dates are also found in your operational calendar.

Projects and Exercises: During the course of the semester, each student will be asked to complete a variety of projects that support lecture and reading materials. Projects range from completing a Learning Styles Inventory to presenting a brief talk about your area of expertise (Mini-versity) to researching and reporting on careers.

Final Project / Exam: Each student's final project / exam will vary. We will develop a model and topic as the semester progresses. In the past, the final has revolved around one of the following:
1. A comprehensive, objective exit examination
2. Community Service Project with paper and oral report
3. A Group Project with paper and oral report
4. An "I Search" Paper with oral report

Attendance / In Class Exercises: Attendance is very important in any college level class. In that light, a maximum of 100 points are awarded for your attendance and 100 points for your participation. The breakdown of attendance points follows:

100 Points	0 absences
80 Points	1 absence
60 Points	2 absences
40 Points	3 absences
0 Points	Over 3 absences

One hundred in-class exercise points will be awarded as the semester progresses and activities develop.

SPECIAL NOTE:
The instructor reserves the right to change this syllabus except for the grading scale and attendance policy. You will be notified of all changes in writing.

OPERATIONAL CALENDAR SPRING SEMESTER Monday-Wednesday Classes

SPRING SEMESTER
Monday - Wednesday Classes

Date		Day	Activity	Assignment
Jan.	22	Mon.	Syllabus overview; Name exercise; Introductions	
	24	Wed.	The River exercise; The Value of Higher Education	Read Ch. 1
	29	Mon.	Motivation and Goal Setting;	
	31	Wed.	Learning Styles; Brain Dominance	Read Handout Complete Inventory **Journal Due !**
Feb.	5	Mon.	The Powerful Art of Listening	Read Handout
	7	Wed.	Voice to Paper: Note Taking	Read Ch. 6 **Journal Due!**
	12	Mon.	Guest Speaker — Lecture on Anatomy	
	14	Wed.	Guest Speaker — Lecture on Theatre History	
	19	Mon.	College Closed for President's Day	
	21	Wed.	Will this be on the test? The Art of Studying.	Read Chs. 4, 5 Read Handout **Journal Due !**
	26	Mon.	Overcoming Test Anxiety	Read Ch. 7

	28	Wed.	Unit Test	Study Hard !
Mar.	4	Mon.	Priority Management: Getting things done!	Read Ch. 3
	6	Wed.	A Celebration of Diversity	Read Ch. 2 **Journal Due !**
	11	Mon.	Video: The Long Walk Home	
	13	Wed.	Video: The Long Walk Home (cont.)	
	18	Mon.	Health and Stress Management	Read Ch. 11 Read Handout **Journal Due !**
	20	Wed.	Relationships and Sexuality	Read Ch. 10 Read Handout
	25	Mon.	Video: Common Treads	
	27	Wed.	Video: Common Treads (cont.)	
Apr.	1	Mon.	College Closed, Spring Break	Do NOT Drink and Drive
	3	Wed.	College Closed, Spring Break	
	8	Mon.	Communication and Life	Read Handout **Journal Due !**
	11	Wed.	Communication Exercises	
	15	Mon.	Mini-Versity Projects Due	
	17	Wed.	Mini- Versity Projects Due	
	22	Mon.	Campus Activities	Read Handout **Journal Due !** **Reports Due !**
	24	Wed.	Career Development and Exploration	Read Handout

	29	Mon.	Careers Continued	
May	1	Wed.	Careers Continued (Guest Speaker)	**Journal Due !**
	6	**Mon.**	**Final Projects and Exam *****	
	8	**Wed.**	**Final Projects and Exam *****	

***THESES DATES ARE MANDATORY FOR YOUR ATTENDANCE! 100 POINTS WILL BE SUBTRACTED FROM YOUR FINAL AVERAGE FOR MISSING ONE OF THESE TWO DAYS!

BUILDING SUPPORT IN and FOR THE COURSE

Regardless of how much you love the course and see the benefits, some students will not like the course, the text, the class or you. We have tried to provide you with several blueprints for dealing with difficult situations.

Students Are Required To Take The Class and Do Not Want To Take It:

This is a common problem at some colleges, especially if no credit is awarded or if the course does not count toward graduation.

    Hints: Be energetic about the course

                        Sell the benefits of the course (page 46 of this manual)

                        Show how course is useful to all classes

                        Make the material exciting and beneficial

                        Bring in speakers, videos, take field trips

                        Talk to the student on an individual basis

                        Let students work in groups, get them involved

Students Are Not Coming To Class:

Some students will feel as if the class is a waste of time and will treat it as such unless you BEGIN with a stern hand. Assure them that you take role and count absences.

    Hints: Stick to your attendance policy

                        Make the class enjoyable to attend

                        Warn students when they are within one cut of "F"

                        Call students at home when they are not present

                        Provide monthly attendance reports to students

Students Do Not Read The Text:

Some students will feel that the text is not important to the class. Many times this happens when exercises are used that are not found in the text.

    Hints: Use materials daily from the text or journal

                        Give pop quizzes

                        Open each class with chapter discussions

                        Have a student summarize the chapter each day

                        Have students write a paragraph about what they learned
                           from the chapter

Students Do Not Complete Journal Entries:

Some students will see the journal entry as meaningless or "busy work." This may be avoided by assigning topics of interest to the student and using the journal in class.

Hints: Have someone share their journal daily

When the journal is given to you for response, be honest and open with the student

Grade the number of entries in the journal weekly

Let them have "free" responses in which they can write on a topic of their choice

Students Do Not Do Homework:

This course does not necessarily lend itself to a great deal of homework, but your assignments are important for students.

Hints: Grade the homework assignments

Open class with a discussion of the assignment

Have students do homework projects in groups

Give exciting and relevant homework projects

Students Are Failing:

Regardless of how hard you try, you are going to have a few students who might fail your course. This can be devastating to you and the student.

Hints: Keep a close eye on grades of all students

Talk with students who do poorly from the start

Notify students at Midterm of their average

Encourage peer tutoring, maybe even in class

Let students work in groups with your assistance

Refer students to the writing, reading and math centers on campus

Refer students to the campus academic intervention office if available

Students Talk To Each Other During The Class:

Few things are more annoying that the sounds of chit chat in the back of the room.

Hints: If you hear students talking, be silent for a moment; this usually causes them to be silent

Look directly at those students talking

Physically move toward them

Ask them to change seats

Ask them to share their conversation

Ask them to leave (a last resort)

Speak with them individually and ask them to help you with this situation

Students Do Not Participate:

One exercise that can be tried is called Mini-Veristy. This is where students actually teach the class. Let them choose a topic on which they are experts. Then, have them present this information to the class. Some will be horrified. Some students will welcome the opportunity. It is great for getting them involved.

Hints: Relate the topic to what is happening in their lives
Be up to date with your discussions
Ask the student direct questions
Let quiet students and talkative students work together
Let them talk about what THEY want to discuss
Be honest and frank with them. Let them know that you are open to talk about any topic

Students Complain About the Grading Scale or Policy

Students usually take their grading seriously. Sometimes, if the course is not counting toward graduation, they have a hard time seeing why grades are distributed.

Hints: Vary your grading system
Don't grade everything
Explain the importance of grades
At first, grade projects at which you know the student will be successful. If they see success early, they tend to overcome the fear of being graded.

Course Does Not Have College Wide Support:

Most colleges have recognized the need for a student success program on their campus. However, if your program does not enjoy the support of administrators and faculty you might consider the following:

Hints: Have concrete proof of student success. Keep records and statistics
Track students through their entire first year and through graduation.
Show administrators the results from student evaluations.
Keep the faculty and staff informed about what is going on with the program.
Develop a monthly or semesterly newsletter
Invite faculty and staff from the college to speak to your class - get THEM involved.
Offer training sessions to faculty and staff on your campus.

BENEFITS OF THE CURRICULUM

Students who enroll in a well-designed student success course gain enhanced academic, career and life skills. They can also gain:

- THE ABILITY TO DEAL WITH CHANGE
- AN UNDERSTANDING OF INDIVIDUAL LEARNING STYLES
- SKILLS TO DEVELOP MOTIVATION AND SET GOALS
- THE ABILITY TO INCREASE SELF-ESTEEM
- AN APPRECIATION OF DIVERSITY
- HIGHER GRADES
- THE ABILITY TO MANAGE TIME AND PRIORITIES
- SKILLS TO BECOME A MORE ACTIVE LISTENER
- SKILLS TO ENHANCE NOTE TAKING
- INQUIRY AND QUESTIONING SKILLS
- A VARIETY OF STUDYING TECHNIQUES
- THE ABILITY TO REDUCE TEST ANXIETY
- SKILLS TO DEVELOP POSITIVE RELATIONSHIPS
- A COMPLETE UNDERSTANDING OF WELLNESS
- THE ABILITY TO REDUCE STRESS IN MOST SITUATIONS
- AN UNDERSTANDING OF THE NEGATIVE EFFECTS OF DRUGS AND ALCOHOL ABUSE
- AN INSIGHT INTO CO- & EXTRA-CURRICULAR ACTIVITIES
- A UNDERSTANDING OF CAREER MAKING DECISIONS
- COMMUNICATION AND SPEAKING SKILLS
- MONEY MANAGEMENT SKILLS
- AN UNDERSTANDING OF COMMUNITY AND CAMPUS RESOURCES
- THE ABILITY TO DEVELOP SUPPORT GROUPS
- A GREATER UNDERSTANDING OF LEARNING RESOURCES
- SKILLS TO DEVELOP CREATIVITY ACROSS THE CURRICULUM
- A GREATER APPRECIATION OF HIGHER EDUCATION'S PURPOSE IN THE WORKFORCE AND SOCIETY

EVALUATING THE COURSE AND INSTRUCTOR

Most colleges require faculty to conduct some type of evaluation of classes and instructors. Evaluations are one of the most useful tools in determining how the course and the instructor may improve. Evaluations show the course's strengths and weaknesses; the highs and lows.

It may be that you have to use a college-wide or departmental evaluation form. If so, we encourage you to use an additional evaluation form to assist you in gathering the data on retention, success and overall opinion of the course. Your college or department evaluation may do this. If not, develop your own. Evaluations might vary from instructor to instructor, but if you are tying to gain information about specific areas of the course, each evaluation for all sections must include a core of common questions.

Questions should be designed to gain the type of information needed for your retention and success reports. Some areas that you might need to evaluate are:

* Number of activities included in the course.
* Were quizzes used? If so, were they useful?
* Were speakers used? If so, were they enlightening?
* Did the text cover materials the students really needed?
* Was the course rewarding in the eyes of the student?
* Would the students recommend the course to a friend? If not, why?
* Was too much or too little material covered?
* Was the instructor effective?
* Was the supplemental course material really needed?
* What could have been added to the course to make it better?
* Was there enough time for participation by students?
* Were class discussion helpful?
* Could the course have used video's for support?
* Was the attendance policy upheld for all students?
* Was the instructor prepared to teach the course?
* Was the instructor helpful?
* Were the instructor's lectures informative and timely?
* Did the instructor support lecture with handouts and examples?
* Did the instructor communicate well?
* Did the instructor follow the syllabus?
* Was the instructor available for questions after class or during office hours?
* Were students given a chance to offer feedback?
* Was the feedback used by the instructor?

* Did the students feel comfortable in the class?
* Was the instructor enthusiastic about the course?
* What was the best thing about the course?
* What was the worst thing about the course?

COURSE EVALUATION

Class_____

Section # _____Instructor_____

What was the most valuable lesson you learned in this course?

_____

_____

_____

Were there enough activities in the course?   YES   NO

Were the guest speakers helpful?   YES   NO   N/A

Rate the course on how beneficial it was to you.
    Not Beneficial   Very Beneficial
    0   1   2   3   4   5   6   7   8   9   10

Was the instructor prepared to teach the course?   YES   NO

Did the instructor make the course exciting and relevant?
                                                     YES   NO

Was the instructor fair in grading the course?   YES   NO

Would you recommend this course to a friend?   YES   NO

What were the strengths of the course? _____

_____

_____

What were the weaknesses of the course?

_____

_____

_____

What would you change about the course if you could?

_____
_____
_____
_____

For our records only (Optional)

Sex   M   F

Ethnic Background_____

Age_____

Marital Status_____

Full or Part Time _____

THE OBJECTIVES OF CLASSROOM DISCUSSION
(Adapted from Mastering the Techniques of Teaching by Joseph Lowman (1984), Jossey Bass: San Francisco)

One of the most important aspects of developing this course and building each lecture is classroom discussion. As mentioned earlier, we have found that students enjoy the class more, learn at an accelerated rate, become more involved in the class and think more critically when the professor uses a variety of discussion techniques. This section is included to assist you in developing discussions in your classroom.

There are five major objectives for using classroom discussion when developing your course. They are:

1. Discussion helps teach course content. Discussion is probably not an effective tool when presenting information that is new to the students. Discussion is valuable, however when assisting the students in processing the information, clarifying the content, building relationships and furthering understanding of the material.

2. Discussion builds thinking skills. Discussion is most useful in teaching students to process or relate the material. Discussion can assist the student in thinking about the topic before they speak. They will be able to hear what other students think about the topic and decide where they stand as well.

3. Discussion reveals student attitudes. Discussion can pinpoint student's attitudes, values and beliefs. Whether the student actually vocally participates in the discussion, the questions posed will usually elicit a response, verbally or mentally from the student. If they answer the question, "Do you or do you not feel that abortion should remain legal?" verbally or not, they will begin to think about the statement.

4. Discussion increases student involvement. An active classroom discussion can move a student from a passive to an active attitude. It seems as if students pay attention for great amounts of time when the subject and speaker shift often. Discussion lends itself to this type of classroom dynamic. Again, even if the student does not enter the conversation, they will be thinking about what they "might" say. Usually, if the questions are posed in an emotional or personal manner, the student will respond.

5. Discussion encourages interpersonal rapport. It has been proven that students want to work for professors who value their opinions and ideas and encourages them to be independent. An instructor who asks for students' opinions communicates that he or she cares about the students' reactions. Discussion can increase the value of the student-teacher relationship as well as the student-student relationship.

SUGGESTIONS FOR HANDLING CLASSROOM DISCUSSION
(Adapted from The Craft of Teaching by Kenneth E. Eble(1986), DC Heath & Company, Massachusetts)

Classroom discussion can be the best of times or the worst of times for the student and the professor. It is still a mystery why some classes have wonderful, thought- provoking discussions while other classes sit in silence. The dynamics and personality of each class play a part in the effectiveness of the discussion, but there are tips for handling and facilitating classroom discussions. Some of the strategies are:

1. Personalize the questions to get the discussion started. Instead of asking, "What is Romanticism?" it is better to ask, "Are you a romantic?"

2. Refrain from personal reactions or criticism. Instead, jot down notes and make your interjections at the end of the discussion. If you criticize or reveal your personal side too early, you will shut out those students who hold a different opinion than yours.

3. Avoid semantic tangles. Let the students talk and see if they can work the "language" out themselves.

4. Deal with individuals who block discussion. There are three ways to move the discussion forward even if someone wants to block it. They are: a) Put questions off and suggest that they be answered later, b) bluntly rule out quibbles as less than crucial and offer a temporary resolution or a working definition to set the matter of issue aside and move on, and c) if the quibble is between two people, step in as the referee and move the discussion away from the quibblers.

5. Use reference materials. When you are planning a discussion, it is good to have reference materials at hand such as the text, maps, overheads, charts, graphs, and physical objects to keep the students on task and show them where they have moved or not moved.

6. Break the subject into parts, consolidate, clarify, and move along. You can be blunt, forceful, yet tactful. Being shocked, outraged, struck dumb or bowled over is a legitimate response. So is humor, praise, or astonishment. Use all the resources you have.

7. Clarify what the discussion is trying to achieve. If the outcome is open ended, it is better to inform your students at the beginning rather than disappoint participants who are looking for firm answers. If there is a time limit, let them know at the beginning.

8. Hold back and shrewdly observe. Let the students conduct the discussion. Participate only when needed to check digressions, clarify positions and give a sense of progress.

9. Constructively, but unobtrusively try to shape the discussion as it moves along. Anticipate the end well before the discussion gets there so that some kind of conclusion can be achieved.

10. Open discussion when the teacher is not present can have some value. This type of discussion may lend itself to a more open and honest discussion of the topic. A tape recorder can capture the discussion and give the teacher guidance for future class work.

INTRODUCTION TO THE COURSE AND CHAPTER PLANS

While you will probably want to devise your own lectures, exercises and reinforcing examples, we are providing instructions, exercises, suggestions, examples and ideas for teaching each chapter of the book.

Chapter instructions will follow the format below:
- ■ General instructions and ideas on lectures
- ■ Discussion ideas
- ■ Exercises to reinforce lecture
- ■ Ideas for guest speakers
- ■ Quizzes

DAY ONE: An Introduction to the Course

After you have reviewed the syllabus with your class in detail, you will probably want to spend some time letting the class get acquainted with each other. We have found that students in a freshman orientation class tend to share more and become more involved with the daily workings of the class when they know the other students in the class.

It is important to start the class by doing some "icebreakers" that will allow the students to get to know YOU and their classmates. Developing an atmosphere of support, encouragement and openness will set the tone for the ENTIRE semester. If the class begins on a stiff and rigid course, we have found that it is hard, if not impossible, to establish an atmosphere of sharing.

PRE- AND POST-ASSESSMENT

As you begin your class, you may want to assess where your students are and how they view their own academic ability. You may need to have additional materials for statistical reporting for your college records. Administering a Pre-and Post-Assessment Inventory could assist you with both endeavors. Have the student complete the Pre-Assessment on the first day of class. Save the assessment until the last day of class when you administer the Post-Assessment. At this point, you will be able to calculate the individual and mean gains or losses.

It may also be advantageous to ask several personal, but optional questions to assist you in determining what groups of people made the most and least progress. Such questions may include:

Sex: Female   Male

Age: _____

Marital Status: Single   Married   Divorced   Other

Yearly Earnings: 0 to 10,000
                   10,0001 to 20,000
                   20,0001 to 30,000
                   30,0001 to 40,000
                   Above 40,0001

Race: African-American
        European American
        Hispanic American
        Asian American
        Native American

PRE-ASSESSMENT INVENTORY

Name_____

Section_____

Directions: Carefully consider each of the following statements and indicate your degree of certainty by answering:

5 = Strongly Agree, 4 = Agree, 3 = Don't Know, 2 = Disagree, 1 = Strongly Disagree

1. I am pleased to be enrolled in this course.   1 2 3 4 5

2. I feel that I am a very confident person.   1 2 3 4 5

3. I feel that college is a positive experience.   1 2 3 4 5

4. I am using most of my potential and capabilities.   1 2 3 4 5

5. My self-esteem is high.   1 2 3 4 5

6. I like myself.   1 2 3 4 5

7. My value system is in line with my class mates.   1 2 3 4 5

8. I know how to set and reach a goal.   1 2 3 4 5

9. I am a motivated person.   1 2 3 4 5

10. I have a good, usable vocabulary.   1 2 3 4 5

11. I know how to cope with change.   1 2 3 4 5

12. I know how to study effectively.   1 2 3 4 5

13. I have an effective system of note taking.   1 2 3 4 5

14. I am a good listener.   1 2 3 4 5

15. I use a study plan.   1 2 3 4 5

16. I know of several ways to study material. 1 2 3 4 5

17. I know how to read a text book. 1 2 3 4 5

18. I know how to relate to my professors. 1 2 3 4 5

19. I know how and where to find counseling on campus. 1 2 3 4 5

20. I am a good manager of time. 1 2 3 4 5

21. I feel comfortable when taking a test. 1 2 3 4 5

22. I know how to take a test. 1 2 3 4 5

23. I feel that I relate to others very well. 1 2 3 4 5

24. I am a successful student. 1 2 3 4 5

25. I understand the concept of culture and diversity. 1 2 3 4 5

26. I am a good problem solver. 1 2 3 4 5

27. I know what I want to do with my life. 1 2 3 4 5

28. I know how to research a career. 1 2 3 4 5

29. I know how and what to eat to remain healthy. 1 2 3 4 5

30. I know how to protect my self against HIV and AIDS. 1 2 3 4 5

POST-ASSESSMENT INVENTORY

Name_____

Section_____

Directions: Carefully consider each of the following statements and indicate your
degree of certainty by answering:

5 = Strongly Agree, 4 = Agree, 3 = Don't Know, 2 = Disagree, 1 = Strongly Disagree

1. I am pleased to be enrolled in this course.   1 2 3 4 5

2. I feel that I am a very confident person.   1 2 3 4 5

3. I feel that college is a positive experience.   1 2 3 4 5

4. I am using most of my potential and capabilities.   1 2 3 4 5

5. My self-esteem is high.   1 2 3 4 5

6. I like myself.   1 2 3 4 5

7. My value system is in line with my class mates.   1 2 3 4 5

8. I know how to set and reach a goal.   1 2 3 4 5

9. I am a motivated person.   1 2 3 4 5

10. I have a good, usable vocabulary.   1 2 3 4 5

11. I know how to cope with change.   1 2 3 4 5

12. I know how to study effectively.   1 2 3 4 5

13. I have an effective system of note taking.   1 2 3 4 5

14. I am a good listener.   1 2 3 4 5

15. I use a study plan.   1 2 3 4 5

16. I know of several ways to study material.   1 2 3 4 5

17. I know how to read a text book.   1 2 3 4 5

18. I know how to relate to my professors.   1 2 3 4 5

19. I know how and where to find counseling on campus.   1 2 3 4 5

20. I am a good manager of time.   1 2 3 4 5

21. I feel comfortable when taking a test.   1 2 3 4 5

22. I know how to take a test.   1 2 3 4 5

23. I feel that I relate to others very well.   1 2 3 4 5

24. I am a successful student.   1 2 3 4 5

25. I understand the concept of culture and diversity.   1 2 3 4 5

26. I am a good problem solver.   1 2 3 4 5

27. I know what I want to do with my life.   1 2 3 4 5

28. I know how to research a career.   1 2 3 4 5

29. I know how and what to eat to remain healthy.   1 2 3 4 5

30. I know how to protect my self against HIV and AIDS.   1 2 3 4 5

ICE BREAKING ACTIVITIES FOR STARTING YOUR CLASS

I FOUND . . .

Explanation:
This activity is designed to get students on their feet and communicating with each other. It is a simple introduction that can be used for many purposes.

Procedure:
Have students write their names on the top of separate sheets of paper. After they have written their names, have them write down one thing that no one in the room could possibly know about them, but that they would not mind the class knowing later on. These statement could be things such as:

    a.   I had green beans for supper last night.
    b.   I was born in Michigan
    c.   I am married with four children.

After this is done, take the sheets and shuffle them into one pile. Put them on your podium or desk and hand out the "I Found..." sheet on the next page. After each student has a sheet, inform them that you are going to read each statement on their sheets but not their names. They are to use each block on the "I Found..." sheet to represent one person.

> Example: When you read "I had green beans for dinner last night," each student should write that statement in one block.

Instruct the students to write down all of the statements, even their own. After you have read all of the statements, instruct each student that they are now to move about as rapidly as possible and find a name to go in each square. They must ask each person a question worded as such:

> "Did you have green beans for supper last night?"
> They should not ask:
> "Which one are you?" or "Which is your statement?"

Give them five minutes to move about the room and find the people for each square. After five minutes, call time and have them take their seats. At this point, tell them that we will now find each person to match the square. As you read each statement, one by one, ask the student to whom the statement fits, not to give themselves away. Have them wait to see if anyone "found" them.

When you ask, "Who had green beans for dinner last night?" see if anyone found that person. When someone identifies Jane as that person, this is a great time to have Jane tell the class something about herself such as her major, hometown, hobbies, etc.

It may be advantageous to offer one point on the final grade for the person who "finds" the most people in the class. This will give them more incentive to locate more people.

I FOUND. . .

THE ISLAND

Explanation:

This activity will allow the students in your class to speak out based on their value and moral systems. We have found this activity to be one of the best ice breakers in the manual. You will find that students are willing to defend and even argue about their own value system.

Procedure:

Tell or read the following story to the class and then poll them to see how many people vote each character as being the most admirable. After you have put the results on the board, let them discuss WHY they voted the way they did and ask them to defend their answers.

The Island Story

Once upon a time, there was an island in the middle of the ocean, far removed from other islands. Actually, there were two islands because a river ran through the island dividing it in to two parts. There was a bridge that allowed passage from one side of the island to the other. On one side of the island, there lived a boy and on the other side there lived a girl. They had known each other all of their lives. They had played together as infants, gone to school together, grew up together, fallen in love with each other, and now, planned to be married and spend the rest of their lives together.

One day, a horrible disaster happened. A hurricane came by and caused much devastation and death to both sides of the island. The boy was at his home when the storm came and the girl was at her home. After the storm had passed, the girl ran to the bridge to cross to see if the boy was safe. To her astonishment, the bridge was gone. She spent the entire day combing the river to try to get across. Her fears and anguish increased with each hour. At the day's end, she still did not know if he was dead or alive. Early the next morning, she began looking again for a way across the river. Toward the day's end, she spotted a man with a boat. She ran to him and asked if he would take her across. He said that would be no problem, but he would have to charge her. She told him that she would give him anything, any amount of money, her pearl ring, anything to take her across. He, however, did not want money or possessions. He told her that the payment would be that she would have to sleep with him. She explained the whole situation to him and begged him for another source of payment. He told her no. She went away and another day passed without knowing if her fiancee was dead or alive. Early the next morning, she was up looking for another way across the river. Still, there was no bridge construction and she could not find a way across. Finally, toward the middle of the day, she saw a man talking with the man with the boat. She waited for him to come up the hill from the river and she stopped him. She asked him if he knew the man with the boat. He said that they had been friends for over 12 years. At this point, she told him what had happened and begged him to ask the man with the boat to take her across. He told her that he felt uncomfortable and did not really know her. He said that he did not want to get involved. He would not help her.

The day passed, and the next day and the next day. Finally, almost a week was gone and the girl was desperate to know if the love of her life was dead or alive. At the end of the sixth day, she went to the man with the boat and told him that she would "pay his price." He told her where to meet him, and later that day, he took her across the river.

At this point, she began frantically looking for her lover. She went to his house. The house was gone. She went to the place where he had worked. The building was gone. After a few hours, she spotted him working with other people removing trees from a building. She called his name. He turned and saw her and they both began running toward each other. They met and kissed and cried and were ultimately happy that each was alive.

The boy began telling her what had happened on his side of the island and that he had gone to the bridge to try to cross. He told her that he did not know the bridge had been rebuilt. She told him that the bridge was still out. He said that he could not get across and asked how she did it. She told him that she had found a man with a boat. She told him EVERYTHING about the trip.

At that moment, he pushed her away and with disgust in his voice, told her that he never wanted to see her again. He told her that she had ruined everything and that he never, ever wanted her to come around him again.

Broken hearted, she left and returned to her side of the island. She was sitting on a bench on the river's edge when a stranger came along and saw her crying. He asked if he could help her, and out of desperation to talk to someone, she told him the entire story. The stranger was outraged. He takes her by the arm, goes to the man with the boat, pushes him out of the way, puts the girl in the boat and takes her back across the river.

When they arrive on the other side, the stranger asks the girl to point out the boy who had "dumped" her. She does so. The stranger then approaches the boy and asks if the story is true. The boy says that it is. At that moment, the stranger hits the boy and beats him to the ground. He is not dead, but he is badly beaten.

The story ends with the following scene. The boy is on the ground with blood all over him, the stranger is standing over him with his arms crossed looking at the girl and the girl is leaning against a tree with a smile on her face.

At this point, you should list the five characters on the board and ask each student to "vote" for the character whom they most admire. Everyone must vote for one and one only. After the tally is on the board, you should begin the discussion and let students tell why they voted the way they did. It may be that you have to play the devil's advocate. You may also have to point out the good and bad in each character such as:

Character	Good Aspects	Bad Aspects
Girl	Sacrificed, giving	Enjoyed boy's pain
Boy	Held to values	No compassion
Man with Boat	Businessman, honest	Opportunist
Friend of Boatman	Stayed out of the way	Stayed out of the way
Stranger	Wanted to help	Resorted to violence

SCAVENGER HUNT

Explanation:
This activity is good for getting students to meet other students in the class. It also allows students to talk about themselves and be introduced to the class.

Procedure:
Simply distribute the scavenger hunt sheet, give them five to ten minutes to complete the exercise and then allow each student to introduce the students on their sheet. Questions could include:

THE SCAVENGER HUNT

1. A student from out of state

2. Someone who is a parent _____

3. A business major _____

4. Someone whose name ends with "S" _____

5. A student who lives on campus _____

6. Someone who works in the food industry _____

7. The person farthest from home _____

8. A married student _____

9. Someone who won a scholarship _____

10. An athlete_____

11. Someone who has been in a play_____

12. Someone who had read *War and Peace*_____

13. Someone who has been to New York_____

14. Someone who owns a Jeep_____

15. Someone who lives off campus_____

16. Some who owns a computer_____

THE INTERVIEW

Explanation:
This is a great activity to allow students to get to know each other on a personal basis and provides them at least one contact in their class with whom they feel comfortable.

Procedure:
Toward the end of the first or second class, you may want to let students group together into twos with strangers. They should not group with anyone whom they know. Ask them to talk with each other and get to know some of the ins and outs of the other person's life. Ask them to go beyond numbers such as, "he's 19 years old, lives at 925 Maple Street, drives a 1993 Jeep..."

They can find these things out, but they should go deeper. They should be asking about majors, life philosophy, goals, why they are majoring in a specific area, their travels, their heros, etc...

The next class meeting, have each student stand in front of the class or sit at his or her desk and introduce their partners. This should not be graded and should be a very relaxed atmosphere.

If you have an odd number of students in your class, you can have three students group together and have A interview B who interviews C who interviews A.

MY SECRET PLACE

Explanation:
This activity allows the student to spend a moment deciding what is very important in their lives. It will also give them an opportunity to see what is important in the lives of other students.

Procedure:
Pass out a sheet of thick paper with a string tied to a hole in each corner of the top. The string should be long enough to allow the paper to hang around students' necks and come down to their stomachs.

On this paper, have the students draw pictures of the things that they would take with them if they were to be in a place from where they could never return..an island, a dessert, the moon, etc... They should not use any words, only symbols, stick people, and drawings. They can put as much on one side of the paper as will fit.

They are not to talk during the drawing period nor during the following activity. When the drawing is complete, have each student walk around the room with his or her drawing hanging from the neck. They are to look at each other's drawings, but they are not to speak to anyone. The room should be silent. After about ten minutes, have the students return to their seats. Ask the students what drawing they saw around someone's neck that they did not understand or that they would love to know more about.

Then, the student with the drawing could tell about the item of interest or misunderstanding. This gives students a chance to talk about their lives and talk about what they value.

THE ENVELOPE

Explanation:
This activity is quite simple but we have had great success with the results. It simply allows the student to look backwards at the end of the semester. It allows them to see the changes that have taken place in a few short months.

Procedure:
On the first day of class, have the students write a one or two page paper about "who they are" at this moment. Ask them to include their thoughts on social, religious, academic and emotional issues. Inform them that no one, not even you, will EVER read the paper. Assure them that they are the only ones who will ever see the content. You will never see or read the paper.

After they have written their papers, give them letter-sized envelopes and have them seal their letters in it. Have them write their names over the flap. Take the envelopes and keep them in a save place in your office. Eventually, the students will forget about the envelope, but you will return it to them on the last day of class.

Have them open their envelopes and write a final journal entry about what they feel has changed in their lives since the first day of classes. You might want to have them discuss what they had written earlier and the difference now. If they do not want to discuss this, don't force the issue.

Another variation of this is to have them address the envelope to a permanent residence where they will be at the end of the first YEAR. At that time, you could mail it to them.

This exercise is great for assisting the students in seeing how much they change in a short period of time.

CHAPTER-BY-CHAPTER IDEAS

SUGGESTIONS FOR CHAPTER ONE
Nothing Stays the Same:
Preparing for and Dealing With Change

LECTURE IDEAS

- Is college really important? Why?

- Why are you here?

- What do you hope to gain from your college experience?

- How can you make the most out of your college experience?

- Change is the only constant in our lives.

- College can change your life.

- Change is coming.

- Premises about change. How and why it happens

- Physical and emotional reactions to change.

- How change may cause anxiety

- Preparing for and dealing with change

- Attitudes that stop or hinder change

DISCUSSION TOPIC IDEAS:

What is the biggest change that you have gone through?
Was it difficult?
Why is change hard?

Why is change necessary?

How is college different from high school? What are the major changes between the two?

Discuss the census earning chart. Does this mean anything to you?

What do you really want from college?

What do you think college owes you?

What do you think you owe your college?

Have you ever been the person to initiate change? If so, how was it received?

Have you experienced any emotional or physical reactions to change since you arrived on the college campus?

What change has caused you the most anxiety? (Use the Change Anxiety Scale).

What has been the hardest thing to let go of since you arrived on campus? Why?

What is the greatest risk that you have ever taken?

Why is communication important when going through change?

EXERCISES:

FORCED CHOICES

Explanation:
This exercise requires the student to make a decision based on values, morals, education and opinion. Some students will find it difficult to make decisions quickly. Some will realize that the way they once felt has changed. Some students will not realize that they have changed until faced with the question.

Procedure:
Have the entire class stand in the middle of the room. This is the neutral station. They can only move to the neutral station one time during the entire exercise. Every other time, the student must make a decision and choose a side.

Read each pair of words and have the students move to the side of the room that you have designated for each response. For example:

Saver	or	Spender
Big city	or	Country
Rose	or	Cactus

You will tell them which side of the room the savers will be on and which side of the room the spenders should be on. While you can begin with simple words, this exercise could grow to include complex, thought provoking questions that represent current events such as:

Pro life	or	Pro choice
Pro Affirmative Action	or	Against Affirmative Action

Are you more:

Political	or	Apolitical
Present	or	Past
Leader	or	Follower
Physical	or	Mental
Argurer	or	Agree-er
Emotional	or	Rational
Tortoise	or	Hare
Falling star	or	Beacon
Clothesline	or	Kite string
Flyswatter	or	Fly
File Cabinet	or	Liquor chest
Motorcycle	or	Bicycle
Raging River	or	Quiet Pond
Screened porch	or	Picture window
Mountain	or	Valley
Fast food	or	Gourmet
Leather	or	Lace
VW Bug	or	Cadillac
Writer	or	Speaker
Loud	or	Quiet

Processing:

After you have read each pair of words and the students have moved from one side to another (or the middle of the room only once), ask them why they are there. What made them make these choices. Were they hard choices? Were they ever surprised by the side of the room they chose? Have they changed in the past few months? Would they have ever stood on the other side of the room?

(Adapted from *Values Clarification* by Simon, et al.)

IF I COULD . . .

Explanation:

This exercise asks students to look beyond their own lives and explore what changes they would like to see in several different situations. It also asks them to suggest ways that this change could take place and what part they could play in the change.

Procedure:

Have each student respond to what type of change they would like to see in each of the following situations:

IF I COULD . . .

Directions: List what changes you would like to see for each of the situations below. Then, list what part you would like to play in the change.

Politics:_____

_____

If I could, I would_____

_____

Religion:_____

_____

If I could, I would_____

_____

College:_____

_____

If I could, I would_____

_____

Home/Family:_____

_____

If I could, I would_____

_____

Relationships: _____

_____

If I could, I would _____

_____

_____

IDEAS FOR SPEAKERS, VIDEOS, MOVIES, REFERENCE BOOKS AND OTHER RESOURCES

Speaker: College Counselors or Psychologists

Speaker: Seniors or upperclass students who have dealt with change

Speaker   Mature students who have dealt with changing roles from mother, or father, to student

Movie: *A River Runs Through It*

Movie: *Grand Canyon*

Movie: *To Sir, With Love*

Movie: *St. Elmo's Fire*

(You will ALWAYS want to preview any movie or video for "proper" content before you present it to your class.)

Book: *Mastering the Winds of Change* (1993) Olsen, E. Harper Collins

Book: *365 Things I learned in College* (1996) Sherfield, R. Montgomery,R. & Moody, P. Allyn and Bacon

Book: *Collective Behavior and Social Movements* (1993) Cutris, L. & Aguirre, B. Allyn and Bacon

Book: *Psychology and Adjustment: Values, Culture and Change* (1994). Cohen, R. Allyn and Bacon

Book: *Exploration in Personal Growth* (1988) Arkoff, A. Allyn and Bacon

Book: *The Illuminated Life* (1995) Arkoff, A. Allyn and Bacon

Book: *Helping People Change: A Testbook for Methods, 4th Edition* (1991) Kanfer, F. & Goldstein, A. Allyn and Bacon

Book: *Choices: Coping Creatively with Personal Change* (1977) Flach, F. Lippincott Press

Book: *How to Cope with Life's Transitions: The Challenge of Personal Change* (1991) Brammer, L. Hemisphere Publications

Book: *Life Changes: Growing Through Personal Transitions* (1990) Spencer,
          S. & Adams, J. Impact Publications

Tape: *I Want to Change, But I Don't Know How.* (1987) Rusk, T. Nightingale-Conant

CHAPTER ONE QUIZ IDEAS

ESSAY:

1. Why is change important to students?
2. What are the premises about change?
3. What is a change agent?
4. What are a three reactions to change?
5. How can you help control change anxiety?
6. What are the attitudes that hinder one from changing?

APPLICATION:

7. Develop a plan to help deal with the negative aspects of change.

8. Identify one area of your college experience thus far (ie, orientation, the admissions procedure, scheduling) that you would like to see changed. Devise a plan to initiate this
   change at your college.

JOURNAL SUGGESTIONS:

Have students respond to one or two of the questions or quotes below in their Double Entry
Journals.

1. "Life is about change and about movement and about becoming something other than
   what you are at this very moment."

2. What is the most important thing that you want to gain from your college years? Why?

3. Have you experienced any emotional or physical reactions to the changes in your   l i f e
   this semester? What are they?

4. "Times change and we change with them."

SUGGESTIONS FOR CHAPTER TWO
Planning Your Dreams: Motivation and Goal Setting

LECTURE IDEAS:

■ Strategies for Becoming a Successful Freshmen

■ Preparing for Success

■ A Winning Attitude and Positive Mental Messages

■ The Impact of Friends on One's Motivation

■ The Difference in Goals, Objectives, and Action Steps

■ Define a Goal

■ Short-term (vs) long-term goals

■ How to Determine What You Want Out of Life

■ Becoming a Peak Performer

■ Reading for Motivation—What to Read

■ The Impact of Fear on Motivation

■ Famous People Who Have Overcome Great Obstacles

DISCUSSION TOPIC IDEAS:

Being on Your Own Vs. Having Parental Supervision
Working Hard Vs Working Smart
Valuable Things You Have Learned from Observing Others
Times When You Have Been Out of Your Comfort Zone
What I Do to Overcome Adversity

EXERCISES:

GOAL PARTNERS:

Explanation:

This exercise requires students to focus on completing their goals by working with a partner whose job is to encourage them and remind them to be working on their goals. The exercise reinforces the idea that associating with motivated, positive people helps them reach their goals.

Procedure:

After your students have written goals, have each of them select a partner and share their goals with their partners. Periodically, provide class time for partners to discuss their progress with each other. Suggest that partners work together outside of class to encourage each other. They might exchange phone numbers and call each other to check on progress once or twice a week. You might suggest that they have lunch together once a week to help each other stay motivated. Work with your students on using good listening skills when their partners are sharing their plans.

INTERNET HEROES:

Explanation:

This exercise provides students an opportunity to explore the life background of one of their personal heroes. In addition, it requires them to use Internet as a research tool. When researching their personal heroes, they will discover the real meaning of the statement, "Extraordinary people are just ordinary people who believe in themselves and get a little better every day."

Procedure:

If your students have access to Internet, require them to research the life story of a well-known public figure—politician, sports hero, movie star, business mogul—and write a one-page report on the highlights of their lives. Topics to include are "Overcoming Obstacles," "Educational Background," and "Events that Helped Shape the Person." Require that students provide Internet documentation.

GOALS COLLAGE :

Explanation:

This exercise causes students to visualize their most desirable goal and to share it in picture form with their classmates. Not only does each student have to focus on a mental picture of his or her individual goal, they get an idea of some of the things their classmates hope to accomplish. A side benefit of this activity is the opportunity to bring all the students together in one shared activity.

Procedure:

Have each student bring a picture, magazine clip, photo or any type of art to class that is a visual image of what they hope to accomplish for one of their goals. For example, one student might bring a picture of the Florida Keys which represents his goal of spending Spring Break in the Keys. Another might bring a picture of a person who has a very nice body. This art might represent the physical condition the student hopes to attain by the end of the semester. Bring glue sticks and a poster board to class and let each student paste his or her picture on the poster board shaping a collage. Periodically, bring the collage to class and let them focus on their personal goals and discuss their progress.

IDEAS FOR SPEAKERS, VIDEOS, MOVIES, REFERENCE BOOKS AND OTHER RESOURCES:

Speaker: An outstanding member of one of the school's athletic teams to share the rigors of becoming a sports hero

Speaker: A well-known local business person who is very successful to share how he or she reached business goals

Speaker: A physically challenged person who has succeeded in spite of his or her physical problems

Movie: *Rudy*

Movie: *Flashdance*

Movie: *Fame*

Movie: *The Terry Fox Story*

Movie: *Hoop Dreams*

Movie: *My Left Foot*

Book: *Succeeding: How to Become an Outstanding Professional* (1994) Harrisberger, L.

Book: *Motivation to Learn: From Theory to Practice, 2nd Edition* (1993) Stipek, D. Allyn and Bacon

Book: *Theory of Goal Setting and Task Performance* (1990) Locke, E. Prentice Hall.

Book: *Work Motivation* (1990) Kleinbech, U. L. Earlbaum Associates

Book: *Motivating Others: Nurturing Inner Motivational Resources* (1996)
                Reeve, J. Allyn and Bacon

Book: *Ambition and How We Manage Success and Failure Throughout
                Our Lives* (1992) Brim, G. Basic Books

Book: *Bringing Out The Best in People: How to Apply the Astonishing
                Power of Positive Reinforcement* (1994) Daniels, A. McGraw Hill

CHAPTER TWO QUIZ IDEAS:

ESSAY:

1   Discuss the concept of motivation as it relates to internal desires.
2. List seven characteristics of peak performers.
3. How do negative personal statements impact one's personal motivation?
4. How does one prepare for success?
5. Explain how hard work alone does not equate with success?
6. How does fear impact one's motivation?
7. Discuss the concept of a "comfort zone."
8. How can one use adversity as a motivator?
9. Discuss the role of visualization in the process of motivation.
10. Describe the complete goal setting process.
11   List the characteristics of attainable goals.
12. Explain why a deadline is so important.

APPLICATION:

13. Design a personal plan for becoming a peak performer.

14. Write a personal goal related to your study habits.

JOURNAL SUGGESTIONS:

Have students respond to one or two of the questions or quotes below in their double-entry journals:

1. Discuss a time when you felt highly motivated. What were you able to accomplish during this time? How did you feel?

2. Discuss a time when you felt inadequate and depressed and lacked motivation.
    What do you think caused you to feel this way? How did you work through this difficult time in your life?

3. If you were another person, would you want to be friends with yourself?

4. Relate this quote to your life. "Your past cannot be lived again; but you can shape tomorrow by what you are making of yourself today."

SUGGESTIONS FOR CHAPTER THREE
Outside Looking In: Devloping Positive Self-Esteem

LECTURE IDEAS:

■   The Components of Self-Esteem

■   How We Develop Self-Esteem

■   The Benefits of Positive Self-Esteem

■   Causes of Poor Self-Esteem

■   Characteristics Which Indicate Poor Self-Esteem

■   Theory of the Inner Child

■   How to Improve Your Self-Esteem

■   Theories About Self-Esteem from Noted Authorities in the Field

■   The Impact of Attitude on One's Self-Esteem

■   The "Victim Mentality"

■   How to Build Positive Relationships

DISCUSSION TOPIC IDEAS:

What Influenced Individual Students' Self-Esteem
Classmates' ideas for Improving Self-esteem
How Self-Esteem Builders Differ Among Traditional and Non-traditional Students
The Importance of Respecting Oneself and How this Relates to Self-Esteem
Past Experiences that Influenced Negative Self-Esteem Development
How Can Students in This Class Help Each Other to Improve Self-Esteem?

EXERCISES:

I AM RESPONSIBLE FOR MY OWN FEELINGS

Explanation:
Rather than assuming responsibility for their own feelings, many students will express them-selves using safe words like "they said" and "everybody is." By not laying claim to their own feelings, they can avoid confrontation or delay taking a stand on an unpopular issue. This exercise is designed to empower students and to help them develop responsible behavior by having them take responsibility for their feelings through the use of "I statements."

Procedure:
Give students an example of a statement where they dodge responsibility.

Dodging Statement: "When people make their own decisions, they are happier."

Take Charge Statement: "When I make my own decisions, I am much happier."

Now provide the following list of Dodging Statements, as well as others that you and your stu-dents may construct, and have students change them into Take Charge Statements.

1. "Everybody says that allowing gays in the military will create numerous problems such as sexual harassment."

2. "My mother criticized my attire, and she made me angry."

3. "My boyfriend (or girlfriend) is making me very unhappy by not letting me know where he (or she) is in the evenings when we are not together."

4. "You are forcing me to lose my temper."

5. "My father is very disappointed in my choice of majors, and it makes me feel guilty because I have let him down."

Possible Changes: (Use your own judgment as to the appropriateness of students' corrected statements."

"I think that allowing gays in the military would create numerous problems."

"Your statement angers me because it hurts my feelings."

"I allow myself to get upset by expecting my boyfriend (or girlfriend) to check in with me on a constant basis.'

"I will not listen to you until you lower your voice and treat me with more respect."

"My dad is disappointed because he wanted me to become the successful
dentist that he wishes he had become."

THE THING I CANNOT DO—LOOKING FEAR IN THE FACE

Explanation:
This exercise is designed to encourage students to tackle things they thought were impossible for them to achieve. It is designed to help them gain strength and confidence through achieving something they have been afraid to try.

Procedure:
Begin by reading this quote to the class:

> **"You gain strength, courage, and confidence
> by every experience in which you really stop
> to look fear in the face...you must do the thing you think
> you cannot do."**
>
> —-Eleanor Roosevelt

Share with students the fact that we all have many fears—fear of failure, fear of being laughed at, fear of disappointing our parents, fear of being alone, fear of dying—on and on the list goes. People are afraid of snakes, tall buildings, elevators, even success.

Have students complete the worksheet below and then go away from the class and make an effort to do one of the things they have been afraid to do by the time they return to class for the next meeting. At that meeting, have them share their successes.

TACKLING MY FEARS

Explanation:
The exercise will allow your students to begin to look critically at their own fears and then develop methods for overcoming those fears.

Procedure:
Have your students complete the following questions:

TACKLING MY FEARS !

● **Make a list of your greatest fears below:**

1.

2.

3.

4.

Now select one of these fears that you would like to work on first and write it in this space:

To overcome this fear, you must look fear in the face. List below the steps you must follow in order to overcome this fear:

1.

2.

● 3.

4.

Before you come back to class, implement the steps you identified and be prepared to share your success story with your classmates.

■ **Having taken steps to overcome this fear, do you think overcoming the next one will be easier?**

Did you learn things from this experience that will make you have more confidence in yourself in the future?

IDEAS FOR SPEAKERS, VIDEOS, MOVIES, REFERENCE BOOKS AND OTHER RESOURCES

Speaker: Person from the University Counseling Center

Speaker: Faculty Member from the Psychology Department

Speaker: Any person from the community whom you know who has overcome self esteem problems.

Tape Series: *How to Build High Self-Esteem: A Practical Process for Your Personal Growth* (1989) Canfield, J. Nightingale Conant.

Tape Series: *The Psychology of Achievement* (1987) Tracy, B. Nightingale Conant.

Book: *Seven Habits for Highly Effective People* (1994) Covey, S. Fireside.

Book: *Loving Me, Loving You* (1991) Schaeffer, B.

Book: *What You Feel, You Can Heal: A Guide for Enriching Relationships* (1994) Gray, J.

Book: *Make An Appointment With Yourself: Simple Steps to Positive Self-Esteem* (1994) Berenblatt, M. & Berenblatt, A.

Book: *Who Do You Think You Are?* (1994) Harary, K.

Book: *101 Ways to Develop Student Self-Esteem and Responsibility* (1993) Canfield, J. and Siccone, F. Allyn and Bacon

Book: *Reaching Out: Interpersonal Effectiveness and Self Actualization, 6th Edition* (1997) Johnson, D. Allyn and Bacon

Movie: *Mahogany*

CHAPTER THREE QUIZ IDEAS

ESSAY:

1. Discuss the importance of positive self-esteem.
2. Name the five conditions of self-esteem.
3. Explain the causes of poor self-esteem.
4. Describe the behaviors normally associated with poor self-esteem.
5. Discuss the concept of the "inner child."
6. List characteristics of people who have a victim mentality.
7. How does one "let go" of painful memories.
8. Make a list of characteristics that exemplify positive self-esteem.

APPLICATION:

9. Think about one of your close friends or acquaintances who, in your opinion, suffers from very low self-esteem. If this person is willing to listen to your advice, what techniques could you use to help this person improve his or her self-image.

10. Identify five positive traits about yourself. Using these traits, formulate five, positive, self-talk sentences you can use to improve your self-esteem.

JOURNAL SUGGESTIONS

Have students respond to one or two of the questions or quotes below in their double-entry journals:

1. Discuss a time when you felt that your self-esteem was very low. What or whom do you think caused it?

2. Discuss a time when you felt that your self-esteem was very high. What or whom do you think caused it?

3. After reading this chapter, what important steps do you think you need to take to improve your self-esteem?

4. Explain the following quote:

"A person who doubts himself is like a man who
would enlist in the ranks of his enemies and bear arms
against himself.
He makes his failure certain by himself being the first
to be convinced of it."

—William Purkey
Professor

Relate this quote to your own life.

SUGGESTIONS FOR CHAPTER FOUR
Understanding Differences: A Celebration of Diversity

LECTURE IDEAS:

- The Concept of the Culture of One

- The Components of Culture

- How We Can Appreciate People from Other Cultures

- How Do We Learn to Have an Mind

- How Parents Might Have Influenced Cultural Biases

- Inter-racial Friendships

- Religious Prejudices

- Sexual Orientation Prejudices

- Racial Prejudices

DISCUSSION TOPIC IDEAS:

Why Jhi' Ming's Colleagues Misunderstood Him
Variety of Cultures Represented in the Class
Values Embraced by Different People in the Class
Impact Religious Training (or lack of it) Has on Students
Problems in Relationships Caused by Different Cultural Backgrounds
Inter-racial Dating

EXERCISES:

CULTURAL EVENT

Explanation:

This exercise is designed to have students experience a cultural event held by an ethnic group other than their own. The activity should cause them to expand their thinking about other cultures and should enable them to take a first step toward developing relationships with people from other ethnic groups.

Procedure:

Locate a number of special events held by various cultures in the local area such a Greek Feast, an International Festival, or St. Patrick's Day Parade. Have your students attend the event of their choice and experience the different culture first hand. Write a list of questions that they must answer by a specific date, questions that require students to interact if they are to get answers.

When they return to class, have the students discuss what they learned. Some suggested questions follow:

- What is the ethnic background of the people who are sponsoring the event?
- How did you find them different from your own culture?
- How did you find them to be similar to your culture?
- What did you think about their native foods?
- Where did the matriarch of the family come from? The patriarch?
- How did their native costumes differ from your culture's dress if any?

Another variation of this exercise might be to have students visit churches of different ethnic groups such as Greek or Russian Orthodox and answer a set of questions.

MULTI CULTURAL WORK EXPERIENCE

Explanation:

To provide students an opportunity to experience a diverse work force, locate places of employment where students can shadow a manager or supervisor and observe how s(he) interacts with people from a variety of backgrounds. Students entering the workforce in this decade will be working with people from numerous ethnic, religious, and cultural orientations.

Procedure:

When students have been paired with a manager, they should be given a list of questions to answer while they are shadowing their partner. When they come to class after their work experiences, they should discuss what they have learned, as well as participate in an overall discussion about how their opinions of other cultures have changed in general. A list of suggested questions follows:

- Did your manager appear to be equally comfortable with people from all cultures?
- Did s(he) treat people from any particular background different from the others?
- Did you see or hear any indication of racial, ethnic, or gender jokes or slurs?
- What was the best example you saw of people from various cultures working well together?
- Did it appear that members of a non-dominant group felt they belonged?
- Were there any indications of high turnover among any one culture?

IDEAS FOR SPEAKERS, VIDEOS, MOVIES, REFERENCE BOOKS AND OTHER RESOURCES

Speaker: Minister from a non-traditional church for the area

Speaker: Person from a foreign country that is not heavily represented by local residents

Speaker: Person to speak on different sexual orientations

Movie: *The Long Walk Home*

Movie: *Dances With Wolves*

Movie: *Do The Right Thing*

Movie: *Boyz in the Hood*

Movie: *Higher Learning*

Movie: *Dangerous Minds*

Movie: *Corrina, Corrina*

Movie: *Mississippi Burning*

Movie: *Children of a Lesser God*

Movie: *I Will Fight No More Forever*

Article: *"12 Companies that do the Right Thing,"* <u>Working Woman,</u> January p. 60.

Article: *"The Workforce of the Year 2000,"* <u>Management Review,</u> August, 1989.

Book: *Managing Diversity,* (1993) Lee Gardenswartz, L. & Rowe, A.

Book: *Affect in the Curriculum: Toward Democracy, Dignity and Diversity* (1990) Beane,
            J. Teacher's College Press

Book: *Racial and Ethnic Relations in America, 4th Edition* (1994) McLemore,
            A. Allyn and Bacon

Book: *Breaking the Ice: A Guide to Understanding People for Other Cultures* (1993)
            Kabagarama, D. Allyn and Bacon

Book: *Understanding Social Issues: Critical Thinking and Analysis, 4th
            Edition* (1996) Berlage, G., & Egelman, W. Allyn and Bacon

Book: *In Conflict and Order: Understanding Society, 7th Edition* (1995)
            Eizen, S., Baca-Zinn, M. Allyn and Bacon

QUIZ IDEAS:

ESSAY:

1. Explain the concept "of the culture of one."
2. List and discuss the components of culture.
3. Discuss the idea of norms in a culture.
4. Discuss the changing demographics of the American workforce.
5. List and discuss several forms of cultural prejudice.

APPLICATION:

6. Identify actual examples of each of the five components of culture: Symbols, Language, Values, Norms, Sanctions.

7. Design a plan to become more inclusive in your behavior toward other cultures.

JOURNAL SUGGESTIONS:

Have students respond to one or two of the questions or quotes below in their double-entry journals:

1. Discuss a time when you have experienced someone who was displaying rude behavior to a person of a cultural minority. How did it make you feel? Did you have an opportunity to intercede?

2. How do you feel about interracial marriages and dating?

3. Respond to this statement: "I believe there are certain jobs that women can't do as well as men."

4. Discuss the positive and negative experiences you have had with a person from a different culture.

SUGGESTIONS FOR CHAPTER FIVE
So Much To Do, So Little Time To Do It: Priority Management

LECTURE IDEAS:

■ How Time Management and Stress Management are Related

■ The Top Line and the Bottom Line of Time Management

■ How the Changing Workplace is Changing Priority Management and the Way We Produce Work

■ Doing vs Being

■ How Do You Find the Joy in Living?

■ Quality of Life Experiences

■ The Body's Cycles—Your Most Productive Time

■ Structured Vs Unstructured Organizers

■ Steps for Effective Planning

■ How to Set and Manage Priorities

■ Organizing at Work and at Home

DISCUSSION TOPIC IDEAS:

Major Causes of Student Stress
Time Saving Suggestions by Students
How to Get More Done at Work
How to Get School Work Done and Still Have Time for Fun

The Relationship of Time Management to Goal Setting
Strategies for Juggling Multiple Priorities
This Works for Me!
Body Cycles and Their Impact on Productivity

EXERCISES:

MAKING A LIST—CHECKING IT TWICE

Explanation:

This exercise will help students understand the importance of making a list, prioritizing the items on the list, and sticking to it. They should be asked to do this exercise everyday for at least a week so they begin to see the value of it. Students should look at their list at least twice a day and should mark off things that have been accomplished.

Procedure:

On the **TIME SHEET** below, make a list. Then put numbers in the outside column according to the importance of the item on the list and the deadline by which you must finish it. As soon as you have any time to work, start on item #1 and work on it until you finish it. Practice this for at least a week, and be prepared to discuss with your classmates. As new work is assigned to you, you will need to re-prioritize your list.

TIME SHEET

NAME_____

Priority	Item	Deadline
_____	_____	_____
_____	_____	_____
_____	_____	_____
_____	_____	_____
_____	_____	_____
_____	_____	_____
_____	_____	_____
_____	_____	_____
_____	_____	_____
_____	_____	_____
_____	_____	_____
_____	_____	_____
_____	_____	_____
_____	_____	_____

PRIORITY CHOICES

Explanation:
Designed to help students focus on making real life decisions, this exercise will force them to set priorities. Once they have completed this exercise, they should be encouraged to practice the same strategies with daily priorities.

Procedure:
Distribute copies of the sheet below to each of your students. Give them 5-6 minutes to place priority numbers beside the appropriate statement. Then have them evaluate their choices based on the key provided below:

_____ A. Pick up heavy parcel. Business closes at 11am.

_____ B. Buy frozen food for dinner.

_____ C. You need money and have no cash or credit cards with you and you cannot write a check. You must go to the bank.

_____ D. Your car is almost out of gas. Go to gas station.

_____ E. Have lawn mower repaired. Repairman promised to have it ready in an hour if you dropped it off on time.

_____ F. Pick up a friend at the airport. Plane arrives at noon.

_____ G. Pick up repaired lawn mower.

Answer Key to Priority Exercise

___4___ A. Pick up heavy parcel. Business closes at 11am.

___7___ B. Buy frozen food for dinner.

___1___ C. You need money and have no cash or credit cards with you and you cannot write a check. You must go to the bank.

___2___ D. Your car is almost out of gas. Go to gas station.

___3___ E. Have lawn mower repaired. Repairman promised to have it ready in an hour if you dropped it off on time.

___6___ F. Pick up a friend at the airport. Plane arrives at noon.

___5___ G. Pick up repaired lawn mower.

IDEAS FOR SPEAKERS, VIDEOS, MOVIES, REFERENCE BOOKS AND OTHER RESOURCES:

Speaker: An entrepreneur who manages several businesses successfully

Speaker: An advanced student who is heavily involved in extra-curricular activities

Book: *You Don't Have to Go Home from Work Exhausted* (1990) McGee-Cooper, A.

Book: *Time Management for Unmanageable People* (1993) Mc-Gee Cooper, A.

Book: *The Ten Natural Laws of Successful Time and Life Management: Proven Strategies for Increasing Productivity and Inner Peace* (1994) Smith, H. Warner Books

CHAPTER FIVE QUIZ IDEAS:

ESSAY:

1. How does time management impact stress management?
2. What is one of the main purposes of time management other than accomplishing more work?
3. How is time management changing as we move from an industrial society to an information society?
4. Name some key strategies for becoming more organized.
5. How does one's body cycles impact productivity?
6. Discuss some priority management strategies for visual thinkers.

APPLICATION:

7. Survey your living quarters and plan ways in which you can organize for more efficiency.

8. You have been assigned a research project due at the end of the semester, how will you manage your priorities to complete this project on time.

JOURNAL SUGGESTIONS:

● Have students respond to one or two of the questions or quotes below in their double-entry journals:

1. Beginning when you wake up in the morning until you go to bed tomorrow, keep a continuous record of what you do every fifteen minutes and record it in fifteen-minute blocks. Evaluate how you spent your time the next day. Identify time robbers. How can you improve your time management techniques?

2. Discuss how managing your time poorly makes you feel when you fail to perform up to your expectations. What are some of the consequences you suffer when you manage your time poorly?

3. Discuss how you feel at a time when you managed your time very well. What steps can you take to ensure better use of your time on a regular basis?

4. Contrast how you manage your time in college compared to how you managed it in high school? Do you see progress in the results you are achieving? Do you feel that you are maturing in your judgment?

SUGGESTIONS FOR CHAPTER SIX
I Heard You! I Heard You! What Did You Say?
The Art of Active Listening

LECTURE IDEAS

■ Making the connection between active listening and effective note taking

■ What is the difference between listening and hearing; which is voluntary or involuntary; is one harder than the other?

■ Is listening or hearing more important? Why?

■ How do you become a better "sender" of information?

■ Review the "Listening Process" as found in the chapter. Receiving, Organizing, Assigning and Reacting

■ Discuss how to become a better Receiver

■ Discuss how to become a better Organizer

■ Discuss how to become a better Assigner

■ Discuss how to become a better Reactionary

■ The Chinese view of listening.

■ Why are there obstacles to listening. What are they?

■ Active and Passive listening qualities

■ Why do we need to listen to professor's key words and phrases?

DISCUSSION TOPIC IDEAS

● When was the last time you tuned out someone because you did not like what they had to say?
Why is it difficult to listen to people or ideas with which we do not agree?
What are some benefits of active listening?
How can we overcome barriers to poor listening?
What is the most important thing you have ever heard?
When was the last time you missed some important information because you were not
  listening?
Discuss the Top Ten Reasons for Listening

EXERCISES

In the chapter, there are six listening activities. Below are the instructions for each activity.

Activity #1 Circles and Lines

Explanation:
This exercise is good to use when making the connection between listening and note taking. It
is also an effective place to talk about how to deal with information given by professors who
talk too fast and do not allow questions during lectures. It is good to point out that if you get
lost while trying to capture the information, the best thing to do is to leave a blank space in the
notes and move on. If too much time is spent trying to recapture lost information, you are los-
ing what is being said at that particular moment. This holds true with this exercise as well.
Explain to the students that if they get "lost," move on. Don't concentrate on what is lost;
make the most of what is happening at the moment.

Procedure:
Have the students turn to the Circles and Lines page. Read the following directions very
rapidly and have your students respond as quickly and accurately as possible. You should read
the directions very quickly and you should not stop or repeat any of the directions. The students cannot stop you to ask you questions.

**Read: "Write your name in the triangle. Put a dot above your name. Draw a circle
inside of the square. Underline your name. Draw a face inside the circle. Put hair on the
face. Draw a triangle inside the circle. Draw a house inside the rectangle. Put two win-
dows in the house. Draw one door. Put a tree and a dog beside the house. Make a small
cloud above the house. Put a hat on the face. Number each corner of the big page."**

Have the students put down their pencils and you should now go back and re-read the directions. After each one, determine who in the class was lost. Talk about the difficulty of listening and taking action at the same time.

Activity #2 Cabbie

Explanation:
This exercise is effective for teaching students how to listen for detail and THEN react.

Procedure:
Students are not to take notes during this exercise. They are to listen as you carefully and methodically read the following scenario. Before you read the story, have your students close their books. When you have read the story, have your students open their books to the Cabbie Exercise and have them answer True, False or Not Enough Information. Only two will be answered with Not Enough Information.

Read:
"The gentleman cab driver had just pulled up to the traffic light when a gunman appeared and demanded money. The cab driver's window was partially down, he let the window down completely, the money in the front seat was snatched up and the gunman sped away. The emergency 911 was called immediately."

Answers:

1. A gunman appeared to the cab driver at the traffic light
   TRUE
2. A gunman demanded money
   TRUE
3. The gunman was a man
   NOT ENOUGH INFORMATION
4. The cab driver's window was down all the way when approached.
   FALSE
5. The cab driver gave the gunman the money
   NOT ENOUGH INFORMATION
6. Someone sped away with the money
   TRUE
7. The money was on the dash of the cab.
   FALSE
8. The amount of money was never mentioned.
   TRUE
9. Only two people are referred to in the story; the cab driver and the gunman
   TRUE
10. The following events are true: Someone demanded money, the money was snatched up, the gunman sped away.
    TRUE

Activity #3 The Accident

Explanation:
This exercise is great for showing students how quickly and easily information can be lost and distorted.

Procedure:
Ask for 5 volunteers. Have theses students step into the hallway so that they can not hear the directions given to the class. Pass out a copy of the scenario listed below. Explain to the remaining students that you are going to read the brief scenario to the first student who enters. Tell them that you would like for them to assist you in keeping track of the information that is lost, distorted or deleted. You will then call in the first student and read the scenario. Ask him or her to think about what was said as you bring in student #2. Then, ask student #1 to tell student #2 what was said. At this point, the class will begin to note what information has been lost, distorted or deleted. At this point, student #1 sits down and student #3 enters. Student #2 will tell the story to #3 and the class will again jot down what happens to the information. This will continue until all of the students who were in the hallway have come into the class and heard the scenario.

At the end of the scenario, ask the last student to tell the class exactly what has happened. Usually, the story will not resemble what it started as. This is an excellent time to discuss how quickly and easily a small amount of information can be lost or distorted.

Read:
"I must get to a telephone as soon as possible! I saw an accident at the corner of 17th and McPhearson Streets. Please help me.

This school bus was approaching the intersection and so was the Honda Accord. They both had green lights. The school bus was attempting to turn right when the Honda turned left in front of the bus. The bus blew the horn, but the Honda actually sped up. They crashed into each other. I thing someone was hurt."

(You will want to make a copy of this scenario for class members who did not volunteer.)

Activity #4 Visual Listening

Explanation:
This activity will assist your students in with intense listening situations.

Procedure:
You will place the following design on the podium at the front of the class. Do not show it to anyone. You will then ask for a volunteer to come to the front and look at the design. You will ask members of the class to turn to Activity #4 in the text. At this point, you will give the directions for the activity aloud.

Tell the person at the podium that it will be his or her responsibility to describe, verbally, exactly what he or she is seeing. They MAY NOT use any body movements or gestures and the audience MAY NOT stop them and ask questions. The student at the podium can say anything he or she wants as long as he or she does not use any gestures. They can say the word square, they can give size, location or any other terminology to get the class to draw what he or she is seeing. This exercise is to get the audience to listen to technical and complicated directions while trying to conceptualize the information.

DESIGN FOR "VISUAL LISTENING"

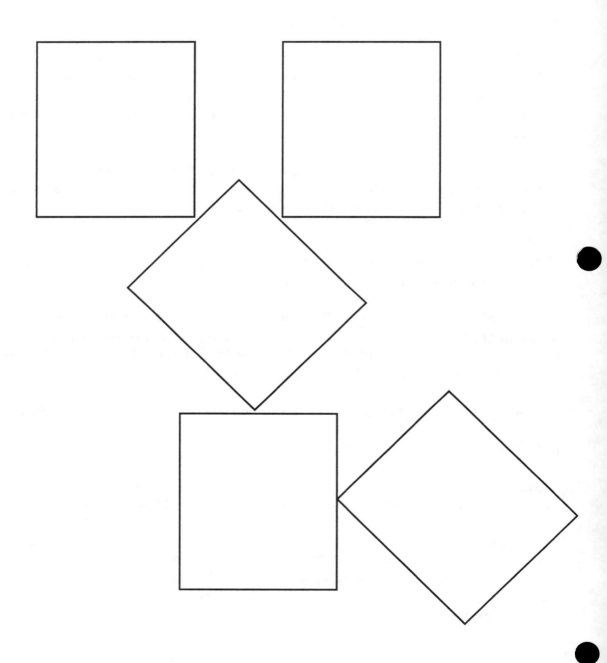

Activity #5 Whispers

Explanation:
This is a fun activity to have students listen is an environment that can be somewhat frustrating. Everything is whispered.

Procedure:
This exercise is very similar to the child's game, Pass It On. Have your students sit in a circle with their books open to Activity #5. You will whisper the statement slowly to the first student. AFTER he or she has passed along the statement to the next person, they need to write it down (and not show it to anyone) in the text space provided.

The reason you will want to have your students write down what they heard is so you can determine exactly where the information began to deteriorate.

Whisper this:
"The way I see it, if you want the rainbow, you have to put up with the rain." by Dolly Parton

Activity #6   I Can Name That Tune

Explanation:
Similar to the TV Show of the same title, you will not ask your students to actually "name" that tune, but to listen intently to a song of your choice and have them answer questions about the song.

Procedure:
Bring a tape player or CD player to class with a song that you have chosen and with which you are very familiar. Before class, formulate several questions that can only be answered by listening closely to the song. As a teaser, you may ask them to listen for one piece of specific information. Example: If the song was "Misty," you may ask them BEFORE the music begins to listen and determine what the singer is "as helpless as." You will ask all other questions AFTER the music has played.

As a discussion, you can talk about the fact that it is much easier to listen to information when you KNOW what to listen for. You will also want to explain that we do not always know what exact information to listen for, thus, we must master the process of active listening all the time.

IDEAS FOR SPEAKERS, VIDEOS, MOVIES AND OTHER RESOURCES:

Speaker: A member of Toastmaster's International

Speaker: A member of the Speech faculty

Book: *Listening, The Forgotten Skill* (1995) Barley-Allen, M., John Wiley and Sons, Publisher

Book: *Listening: Attitudes, Principles and Skills* (1996) Browness, J., Allyn and Bacon

Book: *I Hear You: A Listening Skills Handbook* (1992) Atwater, E., Walker Publications

Book: *The Language of Effective Listening* (1991) Robertson, A., Scott Foresman

Book: *Communicating for Everyday Living* (1989) Ratliffe, S., & Hudson, D., Allyn and Bacon

Book: *Listening Skills* (1993) Schmidt, J., & Cummings, R., Industrial Fair Press

CHAPTER SIX QUIZ IDEAS

ESSAY:

1. What is the difference between listening and hearing?
2. Why is listening important to college students?
3. Chart and discuss the listening process.
4. How do the Chinese view listening? Why?
5. What is listening with a purpose?
6. What is listening with objectivity?
7. What is listening constructively?
8. List and discuss several obstacles to active listening.
9. What are some characteristics of active listeners?
10. What are some key phrases used by professors?

APPLICATION:

To the Professor: Play your favorite recording to the class and have them answer question 11. Tell the students to listen for content.

11. After listening to the recording played by your professor, identify the storyline of the recording; your favorite line from the recording; and give your interpretation of that line.

12. Remember a time when something that someone said elicited an emotional response from you. How can you avoid allowing your emotions to influence your response.

JOURNAL SUGGESTIONS

Have your students respond to one or two of the questions or quotes below in their Double Entry Journal.

1. Is it important to listen to friends?

2. "It takes two to speak the truth — one to speak, one to listen."

3. What is the most difficult thing you have ever had to listen to? Why?

4. What type of professor is easiest to listen to? Why?

SUGGESTIONS FOR CHAPTER SEVEN
Will This Be On The Test:
The Essentials of Note Taking

LECTURE IDEAS:

■ Why is note taking important

■ How to determine if information is important to include in your notes

■ The Cornerstones of Effective Note Taking

■ How to develop and use a shorthand system

■ The Cornell Method of Note Taking

■ The Outlining System of Note Taking

■ Mind Mapping Note Taking Systems

DISCUSSION TOPIC IDEAS:

Do you feel like your note taking system works for you? Why? Why not?
Do you use abbreviations for note taking?
What type of lecture is easiest to take notes from? Why?
Why is it important to re-write and review notes on a regular basis?
Should you share your classnotes with fellow students?
Who was your hardest high school teacher to take notes from? Why?
Why is it important to keep notes from each class separate?

EXERCISES:

NOTING THE NEWS

Explanation:
This exercise helps students take notes on information that will not be repeated, but is already organized for them.

Procedure:
Assign students to watch the evening news on one channel on a certain night. Each student should watch the SAME news cast on the SAME night for optimum effect. They should not record the news cast. As they watch the news, they should take notes on what is heard. You may want to talk with them about organization and headings before this news cast. Share with them that the evening news is already organized for them, e.g...International News, National News, Local News. You might then want to discuss the difference between taking notes from an "organized" professor and an "unorganized" professor.

PASSAGES

Explanation:
This exercise will assist your students in narrowing the amount of information to be written down. It will also help them determine the main ideas or issues of a certain piece of information.

Procedure:
Give each student one 3 × 5 notecard. They can only use one side of the card for note taking. Give each student a three to five page passage from a major work that they probably have not read. Some suggestions are:

> Wolfe—*Look Homeward Angel*
> Hughes—*Salvation*
> Wright—*The Library Card*

As they are reading the passages, they should take notes on the general issues discussed. After this is completed, selected students will share their notes from the cards and try to recount, from the note card, what was covered. This is a good way to introduce note taking from texts.

This exercise could also be done by playing a song or video in class. Remember, they can only used one side of the note card.

OH NO!

Explanation:

This exercise takes some advance planning, but it can be of utmost assistance to your students. Some classes using this text will be focused on study skills. Some of those students may be in transitional studies and this exercise works best for them, although it can help everyone.

Procedure:

It may seem a bit strange, but you will need to listen to your students for several semesters and determine which instructor they find to be the most "difficult" on campus in terms of information and delivery. The instructor for this exercise should be an effective professor, but a "hard" one. Have that professor come into class and give a sample "lecture" from the actual class of Human Anatomy, Calculus, Physics, Theater History, Engineering Structure or any other topic matter.

When the lecture is over, you will want to pair your students into groups of two or three and let them discuss the lecture and compare notes. This will be a fun and exciting way to introduce the students to curriculum lectures and have them actually share their notes with peers.

IDEAS FOR SPEAKERS, VIDEOS, MOVIES, REFERENCE BOOKS, AND OTHER RESOURCES:

Speaker: Professors from the college

Speaker: Director of the Writing Center

Speaker: A former student who might have had trouble with note taking but learned how to take effective notes

Book: *Take Notes*, 2nd Edition (1994) Fry, R., Career Press

Book: *Strategies for Learning and Remembering: Study Skills Across The Curriculum* (1993), Rafoth, M., Leal, L., & DeFabo., NEA Professional Library

Book: *Student Success Secrets, 3rd Edition* (1989) Jensen, E. Barron's Educational Series

Book: *Take Note of College Study Skills* (1983) Bradley, A. Scott Foresman

Book: *Thirty Lessons in Note Taking* (1976) Pirie, J. & Pirie, A. Curriculum Associates

CHAPTER SEVEN QUIZ IDEAS

ESSAY:

1. What are the Cornerstones of Effective Note Taking?
2. Why is it important to take notes?
3. What are some key phrases used by professors when lecturing?
4. What is the L-STAR System?
5. Discuss the Cornell Method.
6. Discuss the Mind Mapping Method.
7. Discuss the Outlining Method.

APPLICATION:

To the professor: Prepare and deliver a brief lecture and have the students apply the L-STAR system of note taking.

8. Listen to the lecture given by your professor and apply the L-STAR system.

9. Reflecting on the three note taking techniques, which would be most appropriate for math, science, English, history and music appreciation.

JOURNAL SUGGESTIONS

Have students respond to one or two of the questions below in their double entry journal.

1. Have students interview a professor or administrator on the campus and take notes on what they learned about them.

2. What is the relationship between note taking and listening?

3. How do you know when something is important to the instructor?

4. What is the relationship between home work and effective note taking?

SUGGESTIONS FOR CHAPTER EIGHT
Avoiding The "All-Nighter:"
Studying for Success

LECTURE IDEAS

■ Why is it important to be organized?

■ The Three cornerstones of Organization.

■ The SQ3R Method

■ The READ Method

■ Mnemonic devices

■ Understanding Memory
   Sense Memory
   Working Memory
   Long Term Memory

■ VCR 3

■ Studying with small children

DISCUSSION TOPIC IDEAS:

Do you really need to study?
Is it important to study in a group?
Can you really study with music or noise? Does it matter?
SQ3R takes so long...is it really worth it?
If I mark up my books, I won't get as much back when I sell them.
Do Mnemonics really work?
Is there a difference between "memorizing" the material and "knowing" the material?
Why is it important to be able to visualize information?
What is the big deal about reviewing?

EXERCISES:

FINDING A STUDY PLAN

Explanation:
This exercise is excellent for allowing students to experiment with various styles of transferring and conceptualizing information. They will use a chart, key word outline, map, flashcard, outline, summary and a time-line.

Procedure:
Assign one chapter from a history book. A short chapter will be more appropriate for this exercise. Have students group into pairs and have them read the chapter in class. Then, you will have them develop a series of notes and study tools for each of the techniques ranging from charts to time-lines. They should transfer the information into a chart, an outline, a key word card, a map, flash cards, summary and a time - line. This is time consuming, but it is an excellent way to allow your students to find out what it take to create each of these techniques and which they fell will work best for them.

USING MNEMONICS

Explanation:
This fun exercise will be beneficial for the class as they get to see some of the clever and unusual mnemonics that their peers can develop.

Procedure:
Find a piece of information that you feel the students will eventually see in the curriculum. This may be Erikson's Eight Stages of Development (Trust, Autonomy, Intuition, Industry, Identity, Intimacy, Generativity, Ego Integrity). Group your students into pairs (or larger groups if you wish) and have them develop a mnemonic for the eight stages that they will share with the class. Each group should have a different mnemonic such as a jingle, an association, a sentence, a word, visualization, a rap or a story line.

STUDYING FOR THE TEST!

Explanation:
This exercise is a continuation from the chapter on note taking. In the previous chapter, you had a professor come to class and deliver a "curriculum" lecture. You will now carry that exercise one step further.

Procedure:

In the last chapter, you had your students take notes on a lecture from a curriculum such as Engineering, Human Anatomy, etc. Have your students take those notes out had let them create a time line, flash card, mind map or other technique to assist them with memory. You may also want them to do a mnemonic as well. After they have done this, have them put their notes and study devices in a safe place. You will once again use these lecture notes and study devices when they are ready to study test taking.

IDEAS FOR SPEAKERS, VIDEOS, MOVIES, REFERENCE BOOKS AND OTHER RESOURCES:

Speaker: Instructor from the Learning Resource Center to speak about studying techniques.

Speaker: A professor from the Psychology Department to speak about learning styles.

Book: How to Study, 3rd Edition (1994) Fry, R., Career Press

Book: How to Study: Suggestions for High School and College Students (1993) Kornhauser, A., University of Chicago Press

Book: Teaching Students to Read Through Their Individual Learning Styles (1986), Carbo, M., Dunn, R., & Dunn, K. Allyn and Bacon

Book: Efficient Study Strategies: Skills for Successful Learning (1989), Usova, G. Brooks/Cole Publishing Company

Book: Brush Up Your Study Skills: Tips for Students and Parents (1995), Amundson, K. American Association of School Administrators

Book: College Reading and Study Strategy Programs (1991), Flippo, R., & Caverly, D. International Reading Association

Book: Teaching and Learning Through Multiple Intelligences (1996), Campbell, L. et at Allyn and Bacon

CHAPTER EIGHT QUIZ IDEAS:

ESSAY:

1. What are the three Cornerstones of Studying? Why?
2. What are some of the supplies you will need to have an effective study period?
3. Why is a notebook system important?
4. Why is a study environment important?

5. What does SQ3R stand for?
6. What is the difference between SQ3R and VCR3?
7. Describe three of the seven methods for assisting memory.
8. What is Long Term Memory?
9. What is Short Term Memory?
10. What is Sense Memory?
11. Why are Mnemonics important?

APPLICATION:

12. Design your ideal study environment.

To the Professor: Choose one small reading from a book other than Cornerstone and have the students answer #13.

13. Read the material provided by your professor and apply all components of the SQ3R Method.

JOURNAL SUGGESTIONS:

Have your students respond to one or two of the questions or quotes below in their double entry journal.

1. Has using one or more of the techniques discussed in class helped you become a better student? Why? Why not?

2. Do you feel like it is best to study your hardest material first of last? Why?

3. What is the hardest part about studying for you?

4. What is the association between priority management and effective studying?

SUGGESTIONS FOR CHAPTER NINE
The Proving Ground:
Strategies for Test Taking

LECTURE IDEAS:

■ Test Anxiety

■ Why do professors give tests?

■ Predicting exam questions

■ Three responses during a test:
  Quick time response
  Lag time response
  No response

■ Strategies for taking a Matching test

■ Strategies for taking a True / False test

■ Strategies for taking a Multiple Choice test

■ Strategies for taking a Short Answer test

■ Strategies for taking an Essay test

DISCUSSION TOPIC IDEAS:

Do you suffer from extreme test anxiety? Why? Why not?
How can you best eliminate test anxiety?
Have you ever failed an important test before? How did it feel?
Do you study better with friends or alone?
Why is it important to learn how to predict exam questions? How can you do it?
Is it important to study class notes and text notes together? Why?

EXERCISES:

TAKING THE TEST !

Explanation:
Over the past two chapters, you have had the students follow their notes from the lecture given in class by a professor of your choice. It is now time to test the students on that material.

Procedure:
Tell your students that they will be tested on the material at the next class meeting. This will give them time to review and study their notes. You will need to develop a comprehensive test using all testing styles such as true/false, matching, multiple choice, fill in the blank, and essay. This way, the students will get a "taste" for each type of question. You may ask the professor who gave the lecture to assist you in developing the test. He or she may have one that they will share with you. This will give the students another professor's testing style to have as a future reference.

IDEAS FOR SPEAKERS, VIDEOS, MOVIES, REFERENCE BOOKS AND OTHER RESOURCES:

Speaker: Someone from the Testing Center to talk about testing strategies.

Speaker: A former student who had extreme test anxiety and was able to overcome it.

Movie: Stand and Deliver

Book: How to Beat Test Anxiety and Score Higher on Your Exams (1979), Divine, J., & Kylen, D. Barron's Educational Series

Book: Test Anxiety: Theory, Research and Application (1980) Saroson, E. L. Erlbaum Associates

Book: Test Without Trauma: How to Overcome Test Anxiety And Score Higher on Every Test (1983), Erwin, B. & Dinwiddie, E. Grosset and Dunlap Publishers

CHAPTER NINE QUIZ IDEAS:

ESSAY:

1. Why is it important to control test anxiety?
2. How can you predict test questions?
3. Discuss five of the ten locations where test answers can be found.
4. What is Quick Time Response? How do you deal with this situation?

5. What is Lag Time Response? How do you deal with this situation?
6. What is No Response? How do you deal with this situation?
7. Discuss two methods for taking a matching test.
8. Discuss two methods for taking a true/ false test.
9. Discuss two methods for taking a multiple choice test.
10. Discuss two methods for taking a short answer test.
11. Discuss two methods for taking an essay test.
12. Discuss five of the hints for taking tests in general.
13. What is the connection between listening and test taking?
14. How can mnemonic devices assist in taking a test?
15. Can you really "overlearn" material?

APPLICATION:

16. Design a program to reduce test anxiety.

JOURNAL ACTIVITIES:

Have students respond to one or two of the questions or quotes below in their double entry journal.

1. Do you feel that tests are important? Why or why not?

2. Is there a better way to assess student learning than through tests?

3. Do you enjoy taking tests? Why or why not?

4. What does it feel like to succeed on a test? What does it feel like to be unsuccessful on a test? Why?

SUGGESTIONS FOR CHAPTER TEN
Getting Along With Others:
The Power of Relationships

LECTURE IDEAS:

■ Life is about relationships.

■ Why relationships are important.

■ How to develop a community during your college experience.

■ Being a friend.

■ Dealing with loneliness.

■ Love relationships in the college setting.

■ Anxiety-Free dating.

■ Exploring human sexuality.

■ Discuss changing sexual roles.

■ Sexuality and personal responsibility .

■ Human Immunodeficiency Virus (HIV) and the Acquired Immune Deficiency Syndrome (AIDS).

■ Sexual harassment and how to deal with unwanted attention.

■ Rape on college campuses.

DISCUSSION TOPIC IDEAS

What relationships are most important to you?

What relationships have changed the most since you came to college?

How have you handled the changes to your relationships?

Have you been able to establish your own community at college?

What strategies can you design to help establish your own community?

Why is loneliness so much a part of being a freshman?

How can you deal with loneliness?

What do you think of the climate surrounding sexuality on your college campus?

Do you feel comfortable with your own sexuality?

Do you know anyone who has been date raped? If yes, how has it affected your approach to the opposite sex.

Do you feel safe on campus?

Do you understand what it means when your partner says "no?"

How do you feel about socializing with someone who is HIV positive?

Do you feel comfortable with your level of understanding about HIV/AIDS and other sexually transmitted diseases?

To whom would you turn if you contracted a sexually transmitted disease?

EXERCISES

HIV ENCOUNTER

Explanation:

This exercise is designed to give students the opportunity to see the impact that unsafe sexual behavior has on a "community." This exercise tends to evoke strong emotion among students and is an excellent way to open up discussion on practicing safe sex and the threat of sexually transmitted diseases.

Procedure:

Prepare note cards for everyone in the class. Write the following on individual cards: HIV positive, infected with gonorrhea, infected with chlamydia, practices safe sex (3 cards), practices abstinence (2 cards), and one guardian angel card. The rest of the cards remain blank. In class pass out a card to each student, instructing them not to share what is written on their cards with anyone. Have each student take his or her card and a pen or pencil and stand up. Tell the students to shake hands with a new person and write that individual's name on their card every time you blow a whistle or clap your hands. Blow the whistle or clap your hands three times. Have the students sit down.

Explain that the hand shake was indicative of sexual activity.

Step 1: Have the student with the chlamydia card come to the front of the classroom. Ask everyone who "shook hands" with this person to stand. At this point, inform the standing class members that they are now infected with Chlamydia.

Step 2: Ask the remaining class members who shook hands with anyone standing at this point to please stand as well. Notify these class members that the likelihood of being infected with Chlamydia is very high.

Step 3: Ask if anyone standing is holding a safe sex card or abstinence card, tell them they can be seated. Have the students who remain standing to write chlamydia on their card and be seated. Repeat this same procedure for gonorrhea and HIV.

For the last leg of this activity have all the students who have gonorrhea, chlamydia or HIV written on their cards to stand. Ask those who have practiced safe sex and abstinence to be seated. Ask the person who is holding the guardian angel card to identify himself or herself and then explain that for some reason there always seems to be someone who doesn't practice safe sex, sleeps around and never ends up with a sexually transmitted disease. There is no explanation, but make sure to point out that although this is possible it is highly unlikely. Have that one person sit down. Have the class look around at the number of them remaining. End the activity by asking students to discuss how they felt once they were identified with a sexually transmitted disease.

IDEAS FOR SPEAKERS, VIDEOS, MOVIES, REFERENCE BOOKS AND OTHER RESOURCES

Speaker: College health officials

Speaker: Seniors or upper-class students who have become successful members of the campus community

Speaker: A person living with HIV / AIDS

Speaker: Psychologist to talk about loneliness

Resource: National AIDS Hotline 1-800-342-AIDS

Resource: Center for Disease Control for pamphlets on sexually transmitted diseases

Resource: Gopher: odie.niaid.nih.gov   for AIDS Information

Resource: Gopher: gopher.hivnet.org   for AIDS Information

Resource: http://patents.cnidr.org/   for AIDS Patient Project

Resource: http://enuxsa.eas.asu.edu/~jvagner/rethinking-aids Rethinking AIDS Journal
            Archives Online

Movie: Philadelphia

Movie: Andre's Mother

Movie: Circle of Friends

Movie: Longtime Companion

Movie: While You Were Sleeping

Academy Award Winning Documentary: Common Threads

Book: Sexuality (1993) Sprecher, S. & McKinney, K., Sage Publications

Book: Love and Sex: Cross-cultural Perspectives (1996) Hatfield, E. Rapson, R., Allyn
            and Bacon.

Book: Sex in Close Relationships (1991) Sprecher, S. & McKinney, K. L. Erlbaum
            Associates

Book: AIDS: Biological, Medical Social and Legal Issues (1993) Stine, G., Prentice Hall

Book: AIDS Information Sourcebook (1992), Oryx Press

Book: Choices: Sex in the Age of STDs (1995) Nevid, J., & Gotfried, F., Allyn and Bacon

Book: AIDS: Readings on a Global Crisis (1995) Bethel, E., Allyn and Bacon

Book: Sex on Your Terms (1996) Powell, E. Allyn and Bacon

Book: The Human Community (1986) Hassinger, E. & Pinkerton, J., Allyn and Bacon

Video: Sexuality and Spirituality in Recovery (1989), Kellogg, T. Lifeworks
            Communications

CHAPTER TEN QUIZ IDEAS:

ESSAY:

1. List and discuss the characteristics that make a group of people a community.
2. What are the basic guidelines in building a new community?
3. Discuss suggestions to help students who are suffering with loneliness to deal
    with their feelings.

4. Name five of the Cornerstones for anxiety-free dating?
5. What are three ways HIV can be transmitted?

APPLICATION:

6. Put yourself in the following situation. Your roommate and you are experiencing difficulties in your relationship due to poor lines of communication and dissimilar backgrounds. Devise a plan to work through this situation.

7. Describe the perfect friend.

JOURNAL SUGGESTIONS

Have students respond to one or two of the questions or quotes below in their double entry journals.

1. "Loneliness is the central and inevitable fact of human existence" Thomas Wolfe

2. Discuss the friendships you have made since coming to college. How do they differ from previous friendships?

3. If you were to find out your roommate is gay how would you react?

4. Do you know anyone who has contracted AIDS?

SUGGESTIONS FOR CHAPTER ELEVEN
Staying Fit: A Personal Plan For Wellness

LECTURE IDEAS:

■ A definition of health.

■ Discuss the holistic approach to Wellness.

■ Being psychologically healthy.

■ Discuss the importance of positive self talk (see chapter 3)

■ Give an overview of the signs of depression.

■ What influences our eating habits?

■ Discuss general tips for eating right.

■ To supplement or not—that is the question.

■ Overview of the Cornerstones for a better diet.

■ The importance of exercise or activity in the life of a freshman.

■ Discuss the components of exercise.

■ Components for how to start and stay with a fitness program.

■ Cornerstones of fitness.

DISCUSSION TOPIC IDEAS

Why should students worry about having a holistic approach to their wellness?
What are some of the health issues students face every day?
In their opinions, what is the most important health issue students faces today?
What does it mean on today's campuses to be healthy?

What messages does society give young people about their physical health?

How do you keep fit?

What are the stumbling blocks students face in trying to be healthy?

What are some positive suggestions for overcoming these stumbling blocks?

What is the difference between being "depressed" and being "clinically depressed?"

How can you encourage healthy eating habits?

What should you do if you have a friend exhibiting signs of depression?

EXERCISES

GROCERY STORE FIELD TRIP

Explanation:

This exercise is designed to help the students focus on how simple changes in the buying habits can have a positive impact on their dining habits. If a trip to the grocery store is difficult the video tape "Supermarket Savvy" (available through Blockbuster Video) is a good substitute.

Procedure:

Check with your campus health center to see if there is a dietician in residence. If there is ask if s/he does grocery store tours. If s/he doesn't give tours, ask your students to watch "Supermarket Savvy" and perhaps the two of you can work together and design a supermarket tour that will help your students. After this exercise is developed it could be used in other freshman orientation classes.

Combine watching the video or the trip to the supermarket with an assignment for the students which requires them to design a shopping list for things they would normally eat. Have them individually go to the grocery store and read labels and make healthy choices based on the information they learned on the video. Have a class discussion after they have all completed the assignment to see what new suggestions they have for their fellow classmates.

FITNESS CENTER TOUR

Take your students to the campus fitness center and have the director give them a tour of the facilities. Then have the students design a personal activity program for themselves and have them keep notes in their double entry journal about their success or failure in being able to maintain their fitness regiment. You might suggest that they pair up to do activities to help increase the building of relationships as well as to increase their potential for success.

IDEAS FOR SPEAKERS, VIDEOS, MOVIES, REFERENCE BOOKS AND OTHER RESOURCES

Speaker: Nutritionist or registered dietician

Speaker: Fitness specialist from the health center or an academic program dealing with exercise physiology.

Speaker: Eating disorder specialist

Speaker: Personal trainer

Speaker: Presidents of student clubs dealing with athletic activities

Speaker: Representative from intramural sports on campus

Speaker: Campus psychologist or therapist

Video: Supermarket Savvy

Resource: The National Association of Anorexia Nervosa and Associated Disorders Box 7, Highland Park, IL 60035   708.831.3438

Book: Physical Fitness: A Way of Life (1992) Getchell, B., Allyn and Bacon

Book: Total Fitness: Exercises, Nutrition and Wellness (1996) Powers, S. & Dodd, S., Allyn and Bacon

Book: Developing Campus Recreation and Wellness Programs (1986) Leafgren, F., Jossey-Bass

Book: Fast Food Facts: Nutritive and Exchange Values for Fast Food Restaurants (1990) Franz, M., DCI Press

Book: Access to Health, 4th Edition (1996) Donatelle, R. & Davis, L., Allyn and Bacon

Book: Health Today, 2nd Edition (1986) Olsen, L. et. al., Allyn and Bacon

Book: Fitness and Wellness for College Students (1990) Burd, J., Putnam, M. & Sevfustini, L., Kendall-Hunt.

Book: The Wellness Lowfat Cookbook (1993), Random House.

Book: Lifetime Fitness and Wellness: A Personal Choice, 3rd Edition (1993), W.C. Brown Publishing Company.

CHAPTER ELEVEN QUIZ IDEAS:

ESSAY:

1. Discuss the importance of a holistic approach to wellness.
2. List and discuss the Cornerstones of a healthy diet.
3. What are the signs of depression.
4. What are some campus resources to help you on your journey to personal wellness?
5. What are important components of a fitness routine?
6. List and discuss the signs of depression.

APPLICATION:

7. What strategies could you employ to improve your personal nutrition plan.

8. Your friend is exhibiting classic signs of depression, what words of advice could you give them?

JOURNAL SUGGESTIONS:

Have students respond to one or two of the questions or quotes below in their double-entry journals:

1. Keep a record of everything you eat for 72 hours. Using a food composition book from the library, evaluate your food consumption for a three-day period of time to see if you meet the dietary guidelines suggested in the text.

2. Discuss your perception of your own personal wellness. What areas would you like to work on? How do you plan to work on these areas. Using what you learned in Chapter 2, write two goals that address personal wellness.

3. Relate this Arabian Proverb to your views on wellness. "He who has health, has hope: and he who has hope has everything."

SUGGESTIONS FOR CHAPTER TWELVE
I'm Stressed, You're Stressed, We're All Stressed: Stress Management

LECTURE IDEAS:

■ Discuss good stress (eustress) and bad stress (distress).

■ Discuss the three types of stress.

■ Review and discuss the signs of stress.

■ Discuss the dynamics of meeting new people.

■ Outline helpful hints for living with roommates.

■ Discuss the qualities of a good stress management program.

■ Discuss the Cornerstones for handling stress.

DISCUSSION TOPIC IDEAS

Since coming to college, what has been the most stressful component of your life?
Describe someone you know who deals well with stress. What do they do that helps them to control their stress?
What is the most stressful thing in your personal life?
Why is some stress good?
Why do some people continue to place incredible stress on themselves through over-commitment?
How can you support your friends when they are undergoing stress?
To whom can you turn when the stresses of life get you down?

EXERCISES

RELAXATION EXERCISE 1

Explanation:
This exercise is designed to help students practice some of the basic relaxation techniques taught.

Imagery Relaxation Exercise—Procedure:
It is important that as you talk your students through these exercises that you keep your voice calm, that you encourage students to get comfortable (loosen belts, slip off their shoes, lean back in their chairs). You might try to schedule this class period in a different setting, perhaps a student lounge that you can close off which has comfortable couches and chairs. Use a soothing and relaxed tone as you talk your students through the following exercises. Playing soft background music and dimming the lights may also help the students relax.

Ask your students to picture themselves at the beach. The beach is empty. The temperature is a comfortable 85 degrees. They are dressed comfortably and relaxing there watching the sun go down. As the sun drops on the horizon, they become aware of the sound of the waves washing up on the beach. Tell them that as thoughts come into their mind, they are to place each thought on a crest of a wave that is receding from the beach. Each wave should take thoughts out to the sea and empty their minds of everything but the sound of the waves, the call of the seagulls, the texture of the warm sand beneath their body and the sun gently touching their skin. Tell them that they are completely safe and free to let themselves float for a while enjoying the warmth and security of their deserted beach. Allow the music to continue to play gently in the background for 10 to 15 minutes and then slowly bring them out of their relaxed state by quietly talking them back to the present.

RELAXATION EXERCISE 2

Tense and Relax Exercise Procedure:
In this exercise ask your students to sit in their chairs with their arms hanging loosely at their sides; their legs uncrossed and their backs straight. Have them slowly tense and then relax certain groups of muscles starting with the forehead, moving down to the jaw line, neck, shoulder area, stomach, buttocks, thighs, calves and then feet. Allow them to remain relaxed for 5 minutes and then slowly, softly bring them back to the present.

IDEAS FOR SPEAKERS, VIDEOS, MOVIES, REFERENCE BOOKS AND OTHER RESOURCES

Speaker: Campus Psychologist to discuss stress management

Speaker: Panel of seniors to talk about how they learned to deal with the stressors of college life.

Speaker: General Practitioner or other medical doctor to discuss in more detail the diseases associated with prolonged exposure to distress.

Audio Tapes: Any good relaxation tape - see local music store or library and select one you like. Take it into class and either open or close your class with it on the days you are discussing stress.

Book: Helping Students Manage Stress (1983) Altmaier, E., Jossey-Bass

Book: Stress in Academic Life: The Mental Assembly Line (1994) Fisher, S., Open University Press

Book: Student Stress: A Classroom Management System (1987) Swick, K., NEA Professional Library

Book: Controlling Stress and Tension : A Holistic Approach, 4th Edition (1993) Girdano, D. et al., Allyn and Bacon

Book: Practical Stress Management: A Comprehensive Workbook for Managing Change and Promoting Health (1995) Romas, J. & Sharma, M., Allyn and Bacon

CHAPTER TWELVE QUIZ IDEAS:

ESSAY:

1. List and discuss the physical signs of stress.
2. What are the three types of stressors and give college life examples of each?
3. Why is stress good?
4. List and discuss practical ways you can relieve stress.
5. What are some of the Cornerstones for handling stress?

APPLICATION:

6. Design your own personal stress management program.

7. Your are exhibiting classic signs of distress. What steps should you take to identify the source of your stress?

JOURNAL SUGGESTIONS:

Have students respond to one or two of the questions or quotes below in their double-entry journals:

1. Describe examples of the three types of stress that you deal with in your life. How are you going to change your approach to these stressors after having read this chapter.

2. Have your students place themselves in a new environment (new campus club, new class, volunteer group, etc). Have them practice some of the helpful hints for meeting new people and report back to the class about their experiences.

3. Make a list of all the things you worry about then list strategies to help you do something about the ones you can correct and to stop worrying about those you can't change.

4. Develop a list of places or activities you can go or do to relieve stress when you are in a stressful situation.

SUGGESTIONS FOR CHAPTER THIRTEEN
Sex, Drugs and Rock & Roll:
Social and Personal Responsibility

LECTURE IDEAS:

■ Discuss why people use drugs.

■ Describe the effect drugs have on your body.

■ Review the signs of drug addiction.

■ Outline the campus resources available to assist people with a drug addiction.

■ Explore alcohol and its effect on our society.

■ Identify the signs of someone with a drinking problem.

■ Review the steps to take if someone is at risk.

■ Describe the negative health effects of nicotine.

■ Discuss the Cornerstones for drinking at a social function.

■ Outline the four stages of drug dependency.

DISCUSSION TOPIC IDEAS

Do you know anyone who has ever abused drugs?
Why do you think people use drugs?
Why is alcohol more accepted than marijuana?
Do you know anyone who drinks and drives?
Have you ever had too much to drink and drove home?
Is beer and wine more socially acceptable than liquor?
Do you know anyone who is socially irresponsible he or she is drinking? How do you handle

these individuals when you are out drinking?
Is there peer pressure to use drugs?
What is the earliest age you were exposed to drugs?
Are illegal drugs readily accessible on campus?

EXERCISES

DRINKING DIARY

Explanation:
This exercise is used to help students to take an up-close look at their drinking habits.

Procedure:
Have the students keep a record for a week of every time they have an alcoholic drink. Have them record the time, place, occasion, and the type and amount of liquor consumed, as well as their psychological state, when they consumed the alcohol. Also, ask them to record any consequences that resulted from the use of alcohol. In class ask them to share excerpts from the diary and discuss what they learned from this record. At the end of this exercise issue a challenge to the class to see who can go one week without drinking a single drop of alcohol. At the end of this week discuss the following: Were you able to make it the entire week? Was it difficult not to drink? Was there any pressure from friends to drink? Did you suffer any physical discomfort from not drinking? Did you suffer any psychological discomfort from not drinking?

IDEAS FOR SPEAKERS, VIDEOS, MOVIES, REFERENCE BOOKS AND OTHER RESOURCES

Speaker: Specialist on substance abuse

Speaker: Members of Alcoholic's Anonymous

Speaker: Upperclassmen who are willing to share their trials and tribulations with drinking.

Resource: National Institute on Drug Abuse Hotline
            Phone: 1.800.662.4357

Resource: Alcoholics Anonymous World Services
            Phone: 1.212.870.3400

Resource: National Black Alcoholism Council
            Phone: 1.202.296.2696

Resource: National Coalition of Hispanic Health and Human Services
Phone: 1.202.387.5000

Resource: National Association of Native American Children of Alcoholics
Phone: 1.206.467.7686

Resource: National Asian Pacific Families Against Substance Abuse
Phone: 1.213.617.8277

Resource: Women for Sobriety
Phone: 1.215.536.8026

Movie: The Broken Cord

Books: Drugs and Human Behavior, 1994, Grilly, D., Allyn & Bacon

Book: Peterson's Drug and Alcohol Programs and Policies at Four Year Colleges
(1989) Schneider, J. & Porter-Shirley, B., Peterson's Guide

Book: Alcohol and the College Student (1986) Goodale, T., Jossey-Bass

Book: Handbook on Drug Abuse Prevention: A Comprehensive Strategy to Prevent the
Abuse of Alcohol and Other Drugs (1995) Coombs, R., & Ziedonis, D., Allyn
and Bacon

Book: Handbook of Differential Treatments for Addictions (1992) L'Abate, L., et al.,
Allyn and Bacon

Book: Alcohol Use and Misuse by Young Adults (1994) Howard, G. & Nathan, P.,
University of Notre Dame Press

Book: Drugs, Alcohol and Sex (1980) Bush, P. R., Marek Publications

Book: Handbook of Alcoholism Treatment Approaches: Effective Alternatives, 2nd
Edition (1995) Hester, R. & Miller, W., Allyn and Bacon

Information: National Clearinghouse for Alcohol and Drug Information
PO Box 2345
Rockville, MD 20852

Resource: American Cancer Society

Resource: Alcoholics Anonymous

Resource: Al-Anon

CHAPTER THIRTEEN QUIZ IDEAS:

ESSAY:

1. Define the word drug.
2. Define and discuss over-the-counter-drugs. How can they be abused?
3. Why is caffeine a drug?
4. List and discuss four of the seven negative health effects of nicotine.
5. Is there a relationship between excessive drug usage and poor school performance?
6. Why or why not?
7. What is a designer drug?
8. Why is LSD classified as a psychedelic?
9. Discuss ways of avoiding drinking too much at a social function.
10. List signs of drug dependency?
11. What steps should you take if you or someone you know is exhibiting signs of drug dependency?

APPLICATION:

12. Your roommate is a virgin. He/she is contemplating having sex with an acquaintance they have only known for a few days. He/she has asked you to help them work through the pros and cons. What questions could your ask your roommate to help them make a responsible decision.

13. You have a friend who has a serious drinking problem. He/she is drunk most of the time and exhibits irresponsible behavior. What can you do to help your friend.

JOURNAL SUGGESTIONS:

1. What advice would you give to your best friend if you found out that s/he had a dependency problem?

2. What would you do if you and your friends were at a party and everyone had too much to drink to drive home?

3. Have you ever felt the need to use drugs because some of your friends do?

4. Have you ever experienced the "jeez, what did I do last night" syndrome? In other words, have you ever woken the morning after drinking heavily and wondered what you might have done or said the night before?

SUGGESTIONS FOR CHAPTER FOURTEEN
To Join or Not to Join . . . That is the Question: Campus Activities

LECTURE IDEAS

■ What is the importance of extra- and co-curricular activities

■ The relationships between involvement and retention

■ The difference between co- and extra-curricular activities

■ Types of campus organizations (personalize for your campus)

■ The Greek System (especially if your campus participates)

■ Honors Programs

■ Media Programs such as the newspaper, yearbook, or literary journal

■ Special interest clubs which enhance academic performance

■ Professional student organizations

■ Religious organization

■ Military and Political organizations

■ Fine arts organizations

■ College athletics

■ How to get involved in campus activities. Selecting a club or association that is right for you.

DISCUSSION TOPIC IDEAS:

Can you be too involved?
Do professional organizations really help?
How much is too much time for clubs and organizations?
Can commuter students be as involved? Should they be involved?
"I'm not good at anything...how can I get involved?"
Does involvement lead to leadership opportunities?

EXERCISES:

EXPLORATION

Explanation:
At the end of the chapter is an exercise called "Organization Exploration Activity." This will be used in class to allow students to learn a great deal about campus activities.

Procedure:
Have your students complete the exploration activity at the end of this chapter. When this is done, have them make oral reports discussing what they were able to learn about different organizations on campus. This will help other students learn as well.

IDEAS FOR SPEAKERS, VIDEOS, MOVIES, REFERENCE BOOKS AND OTHER RESOURCES:

Speaker: Director of Student Activities

Speaker: Vice President for Student Affairs

Speaker: Student Government Association President

Speaker: A student who was highly involved and used this to further his or her career once out of school

Speaker: A member of a professional organization with a student group on campus. This could be a person from the African American Engineers Association or a lawyer from the Indiana Bar Assoc.

Book: Principle Centered Leadership (1992) Covey, S., Fireside/ Simon and Schuster

Book: Leadership is an Art (1989) DePree, M., Dell Trade

Book: The Wisdom of Teams (1994) Katzenbach, J. & Smith, D., Harper Collins

Book: What Matters in College (1993) Astin, A., Jossey-Bass

Book: Involving Colleges: Successful Approaches to Fostering Student Learning and
          Development Outside the Classroom (1991) Kuh, G., Jossey-Bass.

Book: Academic Initiatives in Total Quality for Higher Education (1995) Roberts, H.,
          ASQC Quality Press

Book: Empowering Women: Leadership Development Strategies on Campus (1988)
          Sagaria, M., Jossey-Bass

CHAPTER FOURTEEN QUIZ IDEAS:

ESSAY:

1. What is the difference between extra-curricular and co-curricular activities?
2. List and discuss three different types of activities found on campus.
3. What is there relationship between student involvement and retention?
4. Other than retention issues, why is it important to be involved in activities?
5. What is an honors society?
6. Explain the Greek System.
7. What are "Professional" organizations? How are they used on campus?
8. What is meant by "fine arts" clubs?

APPLICATION:

9. Based on your current career objective, what types of extra-curricular activities should
   you engage in to complement your long-range career objective.

JOURNAL SUGGESTIONS:

Have your students respond to one or two of the questions or quotes below in their double
entry journal.

1. What are you interested in joining? Why?

2. As a commuter student, how can you become more involved with campus life?

3. "Begin, and you're half way there."

4. Do you know someone who is "too" involved? Why? How has this affected them?

SUGGESTIONS FOR CHAPTER FIFTEEN
What Are You Doing For The Rest of Your Life: Career Planning

LECTURE IDEAS:

■ What ARE you doing for the rest of your life?

■ The difference between "being" and "doing"

■ What is the difference between a job and a career?

■ How to better determine what you would like to be or do.
  Personality Typing, Interests, Work Settings, Money, Environment,
  Travel, Wardrobe, Motivational Factors, Value Systems, Skills,
  Routine and Leadership Abilities.

■ How to decide on a major

■ Seven Step Career Decision ladder

■ How to develop a success plan

■ What is a mentor?

■ Resources for learning more about careers

DISCUSSION TOPIC IDEAS:

How much time have you actually spent on your career decision?
Is it a "sin" to be undeclared?
Were you pressured into making a career or major decision by someone else? Why?
What does personality type have to do with career decisions?
How important is money to you?
What part does motivation play in career decisions?

Have you taken a critical look at your skills?

How can you use college electives to help decide on a career?

What part does an advisor play in helping with career decisions?

Do you have a mentor? Why or why not? Who is it?

What are the benefits of having a mentor?

EXERCISES:

CAREER RESEARCH

Explanation:

This exercise will encourage students to get outside of their comfort zones and explore different careers and majors.

Procedure:

Have your students generate a list of careers or majors in which they might be interested. Put them on the board or overhead. Have each student select one major or career.

If two or three students have the same career, it does not matter. Student may chose to investigate the careers they listed, but they don't have to. At this point, have them complete (over the course of a week) the 20 Step Career Research Form found at the end of the chapter. As a part of this project, you might also have them do oral reports about their findings. Encourage them to shadow someone while they are conducting the research.

TEST YOUR PERCEPTIONS

Explanation:

This exercise will help your students test their perceptions about certain fields and careers. It is an excellent way to open discussions regarding gender, racial and ethnic stereotyping.

Procedure:

Before class begins, make a list on the board or the overhead of five to ten careers that are common or unusual. Use the careers as headings across the board so that you can list perceptions under each one.

Example:

Physical Therapist / Garbage Collector / Masseuse / Mechanic / Racer

When the list is complete, take each one individually and have students answer a list of questions about each career. The questions may be things such as:

■ Is this occupation more of a male or female occupation?

■ What does it pay per year?

- Do you have to travel?
- What is the public's opinion of this occupation?
- How many people are in this occupation?
- Is it local, regional, national or international?

And so on. You can develop other questions to ask as well. When you have everything listed on the board, you can talk about how right or wrong these perceptions are. You can then assign two or three students to each of the professions listed and have them research the profession and determine what was right or wrong about the list compiled by the class. This is a great exercise for changing some false opinions that people have about certain careers.

VOLUNTEER BRAINSTORMING

Explanation:
This exercise is used to brainstorm ideas for using volunteer work as a means to establish relationships with agencies, professionals and community service organizations.

Procedure:
Use this session for brainstorming ideas as to where students could reasonably volunteer their services. List them on the board. After the listing session is exhausted, begin to piece together ways that volunteering at each of the agencies or organizations could help the students later on as they begin to make professional contacts for employment opportunities. Discuss how volunteer activities add to one's resume'.

IDEAS FOR SPEAKERS, VIDEO'S, MOVIES, REFERENCE BOOKS AND OTHER RESOURCES:

Speaker: Director of Career Resources

Speaker: Career Counselors (Internal and External)

Speaker: People who have perused and become successful at unusual and diverse careers

Book: The 100 Best Jobs for the 90's and Beyond (1992) Kleiman, C., Berkley Press

Book: What Color is Your Parachute (1995) Bolles, R., Ten Speed Press

Book: Majoring in the Rest of Your Life (1995) Carter, C., Farrar, Strauss And Girout

Book: Changing Careers: A Ten Year Demonstration of a Development Life Span Approach (1994) Gladstein, G., University of Rochester Press

Book: Theories of Career Development, 4th Edition (1996) Osipow, S. & Fitzgerald, L., Allyn and Bacon

Book: Career Information, Career Counseling, and Career Development, 5th Edition
             (1993) Isaacson, L. & Brown, D., Allyn and Bacon

Resource: The Self Directed Search (John L. Holland)

Resource: The United States Department of Human Resources, Washington, DC

Resource: The Dictionary of Occupational Titles (current edition) U.S. Department of
             Labor

Audio Tape: Career Power, (1996) Davis, S., Allyn and Bacon

CHAPTER FIFTEEN QUIZ IDEAS

ESSAY:

1. What is the difference between "being" and "doing?"
2. What is the difference between a job and a career?
3. What steps must one take to declare a major?
4. What is a mentor? How can you find one?
5. What is the relationship between career research and declaring a major?
6. How can volunteering help you make a career decision?

APPLICATION:

7. What strategies could you employ to explore different career option.

8. Design a work experience program to complement your academic curriculum that provides increased levels of responsibility.

JOURNAL SUGGESTIONS:

Have your students respond to one or two of the following quotes or questions in their double entry journal.

1. "Today is the first day of the rest of your life."

2. Is your major your own choice? Why or why not?

3. "The journey of a thousand miles begins with a single step."

4. What are the long-term effects of your career decisions.

SUGGESTION, ACTIVITY AND EXERCISE SUBMISSION FORM

Dear Colleague;

Thank you for allowing us to be a part of your first-year student program. As we told you in the introduction to the book, *Cornerstone* is the product of over 40 collective years of teaching first-year students. In our next edition or the Cornerstone Newsletter, we would like to include some of the activities that make your class a success. In the space provided below, please share a brief overview of your idea, activities, exercises or suggestions. Be sure to include your name, school affiliation, address and phone number so that we can give you and your institution credit in the next edition or the newsletter.

Please send to:
Nancy Forsyth
Allyn and Bacon Publishers
160 Gould Street
Needham Heights, MA 02194-2310

Name_____

Address_____

School Affiliation _____

Phone Number_____

Signature _____

(By signing this form, you are giving us permission to use your name, institution's name and copyright the activity under Allyn & Bacon's name.)

Activity Name

_____

Suggestions, Activities or Exercises (Use additional sheets with this cover if necessary)